My Mountie and Me: A True Story

NORA HICKSON KELLY

Centax Books
Publishing Solutions/PW Group
Regina, Saskatchewan, Canada

My Mountie and Me: A True Story
by
Nora Hickson Kelly

First Printing – July 1999

**Co-published by RCMP Millenium Foundation
and by Publishing Solutions, PW Group**

Canadian Cataloguing in Publication Data

Kelly, Nora (Nora Hickson).

My Mountie and me

Co-published by RCMP Millenium Projects.
ISBN 1-894022-29-7

1. Kelly, Nora, (Nora Hickson). 2. Royal Canadian
Mounted Police--Biography. 3. Police--spouses--Canada--
Biography. I. RCMP Millenium Projects. II. Title.

FC3216.3.K447A3 1999   363.2'092271   C99-920104-2
HV8158.7.R69K44 1999

Cover and page design by Brian Danchuk, Brian Danchuk Design
Page typesetting and formatting by Holly Sentz

**Designed, Printed, and Published in Canada by:
Centax Books/Publishing Solutions/PW Group**
Publishing Director – Margo Embury
1150 Eighth Avenue, Regina, Saskatchewan, Canada S4R 1C9
Telephone (306) 525-2304   Fax (306) 757-2439
Email: centax@printwest.com

Dedication

To my husband, with love in spite of everything

Many thanks to my editor, Margo Embury, who is knowledgable, efficient and considerate.

Foreword

Only a small part of this book depends on memory. Almost everything is based on my journals and account books, on notes made on specific incidents, and on research. Even most of the coversations are recorded in my notes and so are reported accurately. The few remaining are in complete accord with the situations and the conversations that actually took place. Some of them are so deeply embedded in my memory that I couldn't erase them even if I wanted to do so.

Nora Hickson Kelly

Nora Hickson (Kelly) was very reluctant to marry a member of the all-male, highly disciplined, authoritarian RCMP. Nevertheless, she ended her nine years of teaching in rural and urban Saskatchewan during the depression of the 1930s, and in 1940 married Constable William Kelly.

She soon realized that her reluctance had been well founded. There followed low RCMP pay, awkward transfers, housing difficulties, and depressing loneliness while her husband worked ceaselessly day and night. Of course there were good times, too. But the overwhelming fact was that the RCMP usually ignored the welfare and even, at times, the existence of the wives of its members.

Nora, a writer, fought back by specializing in RCMP history. Her first hardcover book was on that subject, and she has become a noted historian of the RCMP. This book is the first part of her own story.

**Previous Books by William H. Kelly
and Nora Hickson Kelly**

• *The Men of the Mounted*, Nora Kelly

• *The Royal Canadian Mounted Police: A Century of
    History*, Nora and William Kelly

• *Policing in Canada*, William and Nora Kelly

• *The Horses of the Royal Canadian Mounted Police*:
    A Pictorial History, William and Nora Kelly

• *The Mounties: As They Saw Themselves*,
    William Kelly

• *The Queen's Horse: Gift of the Mounties*,
    Nora Hickson Kelly

• *The Musical Ride of the Royal Canadian Mounted
    Police*, William Kelly and Nora Hickson Kelly

The Kelly Trilogy

A personal and private look at the men in the RCMP, their training and their service, and the women who support, put up with and love them; Bill and Nora Kelly's stories are revealing and fascinating. This exceptional couple are superb examples of the men and women who helped shape both the Force and the country.

POLICING THE FRINGE: A YOUNG MOUNTIE'S STORY

From 1933 to 1939, Bill Kelly trained and was stationed with the RCMP in Saskatchewan. During frontier postings, with patrols on horseback and no telephone, he dealt with bootleggers, illicit stills, cattle and horse theft and insanity. He patrolled on horseback, by democrat, canoe, snowshoes, police car and float plane. Hardship and adventure, life in a pioneer land – the daily routine of a frontier RCMP constable, the specific and absorbing details of Bill and Nora Kelly's fine book brings this time period alive.

POLICING IN WARTIME: ONE MOUNTIE'S STORY

While Canadian service personnel made heroic sacrifices battling the Nazis, other Canadians on the home front were sabotaging the war effort. Bill Kelly, as part of the RCMP Black Market Squad in Toronto, investigated and prosecuted black market activity and security risks in southern Ontario during World War II. Bill Kelly, Former Deputy Commissioner and Director of Security and Intelligence of the RCMP, and co-author Nora Kelly's accurate account of this time period deals with blackmail, fraud, spies, sabotage, illegal gold exports, foreign exchange, gasoline and other rationing abuses. These offences and subsequent RCMP investigations were repeated throughout Canada during the war.

MY MOUNTIE AND ME: A TRUE STORY

Nora Hickson Kelly married a man, not the Force – or so she thought! At times the RCMP became a demanding third partner in the Kelly marriage. One woman's story, Nora Kelly's book details the experiences of many RCMP wives. A determined and talented writer, Nora became a free-lance journalist. Her inside knowledge of the RCMP made her the ideal author and co-author of several books on the Force. Her keen observations and astonishing memory make her writing true and vital. This important book provides a glimpse into the lives of the Kellys and of many wives and their mounties.

O_{NE}

"I f you'll be our accompanist for the festival, Miss Hickson, I'll get a good-looking young mountie to drive you home from each choir practice."

Alex Kevan, choirmaster of the Anglican church in the small city of North Battleford, Saskatchewan, was trying to persuade me in person to do what I had already refused by telephone. That Friday afternoon he had driven out to the Provincial Mental Hospital, three miles out of town, where I taught children of the hospital staff. He had arrived so promptly at the end of the school day that I still wore my smock, a three-quarter-length cover-up of small red and white checks, with big red and black toy drums for pockets. Now the slight, blonde, rather effeminate young man and I sat perched on small desks in my Grades 1 to 4 classroom as he pleaded with me to change my mind.

He made his mountie offer as if playing his top-ranking trump card. After all, many young women in North Battleford would have jumped at the chance to get to know a young mountie. In those days, "young mountie" usually also meant "eligible bachelor". Mr. Kevan obviously expected that I would accept his offer with gratitude.

To me, however, "young mountie" meant something quite different from what Mr. Kevan had in mind. At that time, in the spring of 1937, the great depression of the 1930s still raged. Thousands of young men were unemployed, and many of them rode the freight trains illegally, hoping to find work and sustenance somewhere, anywhere. My heart ached for them. I resented the fact that mounties searched the freight trains for illegal riders and ordered them off, leaving them helpless and hopeless. I wanted nothing to do with any member of an all-male, authoritarian organization that I perceived as the strong-arm authority of an uncaring federal government. I was not the least bit tempted by Mr. Kevan's offer of drives with a mountie.

"I'm sorry," I said, "but I'm accompanying the North Battleford Ladies' Chorus, and my mother and her friend in their duet. That means bus trips to town several nights a week. And of course I have my own school chorus. I simply can't take on anything else."

The choir leader looked dejected. "You're our last hope," he murmured sorrowfully. "If I can't find an accompanist, we can't enter the festival."

I knew he was right. One of the choir's festival pieces had a difficult piano accompaniment that the church organist couldn't play. A noted pianist from across the river in the small town of Battleford had agreed to fill in. However, she was not used to accompanying. At the first rehearsal she had given up.

I knew, too, that what made the choir especially eager to compete was that for the past few years they had won the shield in their class. They had expected that in the festival of 1937 they would win again. In those bleak, depressed 1930s there were few if any cultural events in rural and small town Saskatchewan. Winning a shield or a cup at North Battleford's annual music festival meant a moment of glory and a year of prestige. I could imagine how St. Paul's choir felt.

"I'm really sorry I can't help you," I said.

"The whole choir will be sorry," Mr. Kevan sighed, "including your mother."

My mother! She taught at King Street School in North Battleford, and was in St. Paul's choir. She would be as disappointed as anyone at being unable to compete in the festival. Yet she hadn't tried to persuade me to be their festival accompanist. Instead, she had warned me not to undertake too much.

"You mustn't get so tired that your back gives out again," she had advised me.

Dear Mom! She always considered my welfare ahead of everything else. After my father died she had left the security of her position as headmistress of a school in England, and we had emigrated to a recently settled area in north-central Saskatchewan, where she would teach and be near her parents and my three uncles who had pioneered there. Her main reason for emigrating, however, was that she believed Canada would provide me with more opportunity than

I would have in class-conscious, restrictive England. During our first three years in Canada, when we endured appalling and unexpected hardships, my uncomplaining mother had always protected me from them to the best of her ability.

Moreover, even during that poverty-stricken period, she had given me whatever cultural advantages she could. Even my proficiency at the piano had grown from her early encouragement, when she arranged for my first piano lessons when I was eight years old. Unfortunately, that was in England during World War I. I became critically ill with trench mouth and Spanish flu. I didn't fully recover until the next year, when we emigrated to Canada.

During the first two years my mother taught in a one-room school at Brightsand Lake, a very primitive area. During our second year there we lived in a one-room, sod-roofed log cabin, with our minimal furniture augmented by packing crates and apple boxes. But we had a piano! When my mother learned that an overly-optimistic homesteader could no longer afford the five-dollar-a-month installments on his piano, she took over the payments and the piano. She also took over, on monthly payments, his long-term subscription to *Étude* magazine, a substantial American publication that contained articles on music and musicians, and piano pieces grade by half grades from Grade 1 to Grade 6.

The piano was our most precious possession. During the spring thaw of 1921, our first in the log cabin, and later when the rains came, our first concern was to protect the piano from the water that leaked through our sod roof. Quickly my mother grabbed a blanket from the bed, folded it on the run, and threw it over the piano. In one continuous movement she dashed to get her neatly rolled black English umbrella, unfurled it with a flourish, and propped it in place on the blanket. Meanwhile I hurried to gather all the empty lard and jam pails, and even the smaller tomato and baking powder tins we had purposely saved. Then the two of us placed them in strategic places on the piano, the bed, the cabin trunk, and so on, and hoped for the best.

Just as my mother bought the piano and the *Étude* magazines with monthly payments, she also bought a set of *The Book of Knowledge*, about ten big books I seem to remember, from a travelling salesman. They resembled a junior encyclopaedia, and contained intriguing information on almost every subject considered important in those days. As my mother had no doubt planned, I spent many happy hours, oblivious to my dreary surroundings, engrossed not only in sections on fairy tales and children's literature, but also those on English literature, science and astronomy, the latter of which fascinated me most.

During our difficult three years in this primitive homestead area of Saskatchewan, my mother shielded me not only from my dreary indoor surroundings, but also from the outdoor hardships. This was especially notable during our year in the log cabin, when our nearest supply of water was at the farmer's pump half a mile away. Although my uncles filled our water pails when they came at weekends to check on our welfare, sometimes they couldn't come. Then we had to get the water ourselves.

In the mosquito-infested spring of that dreadful log cabin year of 1921, although I was eleven by then, my mother insisted on fetching water alone. In those days women didn't wear slacks, so she hoped to outwit the fierce insects by wearing her longest, heaviest skirt and matching black jacket. She covered her head and ears with a gray woollen scarf, and put on her winter gloves.

In one hand she carried a large pail. In the other she grasped a fistful of young poplar branches with their delicate froth of spring leaves. These she waved frantically, trying to fight off the swarms of ravenous, whining insects as she plodded over the half mile of dusty trail that led through dense bush to the farm. And of course she faced the same swarms all the way home.

In spite of her best efforts, the mosquitoes inflicted painful stings on her arms, legs and face, causing them to swell alarmingly. She dabbed the bites with a cube of laundry blueing that the sympathetic farmer's wife recommended, and tried to carry on as usual. On one occasion, however, she was so poisoned that she had to go to bed for several days.

When we moved to North Battleford, where she taught at King Street School, I had piano lessons until I was fed up with having to practice the same pieces over and over for exams. At that point I was allowed to stop taking lessons and to play and learn whatever I liked. After that I had dancing lessons. My mother paid for them by playing the piano for the Saturday morning class, thus giving up precious time she needed for Saturday shopping, cleaning, cooking, washing and ironing, most of which she refused to let me share.

In fact, my mother had provided me with the privilege of whatever early learning I'd had. How could I deprive her of the simple pleasure of St. Paul's choir competing in the music festival? How could I be such an ingrate? On the other hand, I was apprehensive about undertaking more festival activities.

I was silent as Mr. Kevan stood up, pulled down the jacket of his neat navy suit, and picked up his music satchel that leaned, unopened, against a desk. As he moved toward my classroom door, his shoulders drooped and he seemed to have difficulty forcing a smile as he said goodbye.

By the time his hand grasped the doorknob I knew what I must do. "I've changed my mind," I said. "I'll be your accompanist."

"That's wonderful!" Mr. Kevan beamed, straightening his slight figure and throwing back his shoulders. "Wonderful!" he repeated. Quickly he opened his satchel, took out a folder of music, and happily waved it toward me. "You'll probably want to try this out tonight," he smiled. "We'll have a special practice tomorrow afternoon at two o'clock."

As we walked out into the bright spring sunshine and the rustle of young poplar leaves in the constant Saskatchewan breeze, Mr. Kevan looked as if he might at any time break into a hop, skip and jump.

"I don't know how to thank you," he said earnestly as we reached his black Chevrolet sedan. He got into the car, wound down his left front window, and leaned out to give me a warm handshake. "And of course the young mountie will drive you home," he said, as if he were repaying me for my promised help. Then he rolled up the window and drove away.

As I walked to the nearby red brick apartment block where I shared a basement suite with three nurses, I thought of how surprised Mr. Kevan would be if he knew how I felt about mounties. Anyway, I was glad I had agreed to accompany his choir, and that evening when I telephoned my mother, her pleasure convinced me that I had indeed done the right thing.

The next afternoon I went to town by bus for the special Saturday practice with St. Paul's choir. It went well, and everyone was happy. After the practice Mr. Kevan kept his promise and asked Constable William Kelly to drive me back to the hospital.

I could see that Constable Kelly was taken by surprise, but he couldn't very well refuse. So after I said goodbye to my mother, we got into his well-polished black Model A Ford coupé, and drove decorously along tree-lined sunlit streets to the edge of town.

At first we drove along without speaking. Constable Kelly sat as upright and silent in his civilian spring coat as I presumed he would have done in uniform. I, in my red felt hat and my gray and red plaid suit with slightly flared three-quarter-length jacket, also sat upright and silent. I couldn't think of anything I wanted to talk about, and apparently neither could he. Anyone scrutinizing us would have categorized us as a younger, better-dressed version of the tight-lipped couple in Grant Wood's *American Gothic* painting.

I broke the silence, however, as we reached the gravel highway and the coupé began to bump alarmingly.

"Don't you find this car a bit rough, Constable Kelly?" I asked.

"It's not the car, Miss Hickson," he replied curtly. "It's the road."

I didn't believe him. But I could tell I'd better not insult his well-preserved 1930 coupé again. Meanwhile, other drivers and men at service stations along the highway waved vigorously as we bumped past. Smiling, Constable Kelly responded to each wave with one of his own.

"They're very friendly in this district," he said. "I didn't think they'd know me yet. I've only been in North Battleford about two months."

We bumped and waved for two miles. Then the bumps became great humps.

"Shouldn't you check something?" I dared to suggest.

"It's only the road!" Constable Kelly rebuked me sharply. But he got out to look.

I got out, too. I saw that not only had we had a flat tire, as all those friendly people had tried to warn us, but now the tire and tube had come off. Ever since the bumps turned to humps, we had been travelling on the rim.

"We lost a tire, that's all," Constable Kelly remarked nonchalantly. He took off his beige tweed coat, folded it neatly, and carefully laid it on the seat of the car.

Quickly and efficiently he pumped up the spare tire and put it on. Then without comment we drove back along the highway and retrieved, first the inner tube, then the tire.

When, a short time later, Constable Kelly politely deposited me at the front of the apartment block where I lived, he still had not complained about the trouble he'd had. I admitted to myself that he seemed unusually self-reliant and mature. Nevertheless, I had no desire to get to know Mounted Policeman Kelly any better.

1938, Spruce Bluff. Bill and I pose with his 1930 Ford coupé while visiting my Light relatives on their farm. I am wearing the grey and red plaid suit I wore during the lost tire incident.

1937, North Battleford. Bill wearing his tweed spring coat.

TWO

A few minutes later I was lying on my bed, relaxing till suppertime. Then I would have my evening meal, as I had all my meals, with the family of a friendly hospital attendant.

As I lay there on the hospital-type bed with the white enamelled metal frame, I merely dozed. But if, instead, I had tried to understand why I felt ultra-cool toward RCMP Constable Kelly, the probing would have covered half my lifetime of twenty-six years.

In fact, my resentment of male authority came partly from my feelings of inferiority in being female.

As early as age thirteen, in Grade 8, I was well aware of that stigma. A boy in the class was disgruntled because, after my widowed mother and I moved to North Battleford, I consistently displaced him from first place on the monthly honour roll. When my teacher said I would make a good lawyer, Walter laughed at the idea.

"You'll never make it," he scoffed. "Even the best chefs are men."

Walter's remark didn't surprise me. In my limited world in 1923, men held all the most important positions. Incidentally, although World War I had forced Canada's federal politicians to recognize the value of women's war work, and in 1918 women had been given the right to vote, the general impression remained that women were inferior beings.

That impression prevailed during my four years in high school. Even though I was able to prove that one female, at least, was not inferior by winning each year's medal for scholastic achievement, I didn't think of that at the time.

After high school I attended Normal (Teacher Training) School in Saskatoon. My male history teacher seemed to think that the female students had no right to hold any opinion that differed from his. When I questioned the relative value of the elaborate, time-consuming history charts that he insisted all teachers must make, he shouted at me and slapped his yardstick on my desk half a dozen times. Some of my classmates thought he would expel me, or at least bar me from his classes. But he did neither, and I was graduated with the other students in June 1929.

During the next nine years, when I taught in elementary schools in Saskatchewan, I frequently felt the weight of male authority. My problems began at my first school, and involved the board of three male trustees.

The school was at McLaren, a prosperous farming area in the rolling parkland of west-central Saskatchewan, not yet affected by the depression soon to plague Canada. Although I had thirty-eight pupils in Grades 1 to 7, I was happy there. I liked the children and the people of the district, and they liked me. I had good inspector's reports, and I'd put on a splendid Christmas concert. I knew I had done well, and I hoped to stay at McLaren.

The problem with the trustees arose because the school had a teacherage, a little building on the school grounds, and I was expected to live in it.

I lived in it from the beginning of the school year in September 1929 to Christmas, but I found living there a dreadful hardship. The uninsulated building, of one-inch lumber and exposed two-by-fours, was so bitterly cold from the end of September that I had to get up several times in the night to stoke the coal-burning cookstove. I had to cook for myself, but I didn't know how to cook. I also had to do my own laundry, using water ladled with a tin dipper from a barrel into the reservoir on the side of the cookstove. Then I re-ladled it into a galvanized metal washtub. I used a corrugated washboard, wrung clothes and bedding by hand, and dried things on an outdoor line in all weathers. During my four months in the teacherage, at age nineteen, I also prepared lessons for seven grades, and lost ten pounds.

When I went to McLaren I was also expected to do the janitor work in the school, and to light and tend the school furnace. For those services fifty dollars would be added to my annual salary of $1,000. On my first day there, however, I turned the janitor and furnace work over to two pupils whose family needed the money.

At Christmas time a friendly Finnish family offered to have me as a boarder. I accepted with gratitude, and enjoyed every moment I spent with the Johnson family. Motherly Mrs. Johnson and her daughter Ruth were splendid cooks. Everyone was musical, and Ruth was a trained soprano. Music reigned in the evenings and at weekends. I hoped to teach at McLaren and live with the Johnsons for many years.

The school board, however, had other plans for me. I could stay, they said, but only if I lived in the teacherage. Otherwise the building would deteriorate. I simply couldn't go back to living in the teacherage. Reluctantly I resigned and moved on.

In September 1930 I went to my second school. It was in north-central Saskatchewan at Brightsand Lake, my mother's first school in Canada. The district, well-wooded with poplars and evergreens, had become a fully settled farming district. The soil, however, was not very fertile, and crops were usually poor. And now, the onset of the 1930s' depression resulted in low prices for their meagre crops of wheat, oats and flax.

By then the depression was also creating hard times for teachers. I was well aware of my luck in having obtained a second school without delay, and one with no teacherage. I was lucky, too, that I now had only twenty-four pupils, although they were in Grades 1 through 8, and my salary was much lower than at McLaren.

Compared with the farmers at Brightsand Lake I was extremely fortunate. My own and my mother's background of hardship in that same district created in me a disturbing empathy for my pupils and the adults of the district. In fact, my experience of poverty at Brightsand Lake had as lasting an influence on me as my resentment of intrusive male authority.

I became very sympathetic to one of my Grade 1 pupils. He was six-year-old Ray, a likeable little boy with well-brushed brown hair, sparkling blue eyes, and a keen desire to learn to read immediately. To my dismay, I discovered that Ray faced the oncoming bitter Saskatchewan winter without a warm coat. I boarded with his farming parents, so I knew that in spite of their endless work, they couldn't afford to buy a coat for Ray. I offered to make one for him.

I felt confident that I could make the coat. From the time I was fifteen till I was graduated from high school, I had made many of my own clothes. The money that bought the materials came from the $2.50 a week I earned by playing the piano for the choir of the impoverished Continuing Presbyterians. They had refused to unite with the other Presbyterians and the Methodists in the newly formed United Church. My earnings had allowed me to buy or make all my own clothes, and my crowning sewing achievement had been a spring coat.

That coat was highly unsuitable for a Grade-12 girl in the small city of North Battleford. But wearing it eased the deep-rooted sense of inadequacy and inferiority that had plagued me most of my life.

I had made my beautiful garment from rich powder-blue wool gabardine and best-quality creamy beige lining, both materials bought through Eaton's catalogue. The plain collar of the coat extended to a wide, hem-length scarf edged at the wide end with three-inch "red fox" (dyed-rabbit) fur, also from Eaton's catalogue. During my last year in high school and one year at Normal School, the coat gave me the security of looking well-dressed. I was slim, my five-foot six-inch frame was considered tall in those days, and I had naturally good posture. I felt the equal of anyone when I flung the "fox"-edged scarf over my left shoulder as I had seen elegant women do in the movies. In fact, wearing my smart clothes was like acting in a play, as I had done each year in high school: my own identity was submerged in another.

Unfortunately, that lovely coat was even less suitable for trudging along dusty roads to a one-room school, two miles away from the farm where I knew I was to board at Brightsand Lake. Before I left home I took the coat apart, had the pieces dyed navy blue, and redid it without the scarf-collar.

Obviously I felt qualified to make a coat for Ray. I began by cutting suitable pieces from the stylish dark-gray overcoat that his immigrant father had brought, optimistically, from Holland. I sewed the pieces together on an old-fashioned treadle machine that Ray's English mother had bought, through the ubiquitous Eaton's catalogue, in an earlier year when crops were reasonably good and prices were high.

Ray's coat was a great success. In appreciation, Ray used the scraps to make me a unique pair of mittens. He sewed the pieces together with an over-sized darning needle and gray darning wool, using half-inch stitches and leaving all seams exposed on the outside of the mittens. I kept them for years, remembering Ray's shining eyes as he presented me with his gift of gratitude.

At the same school, twelve-year-old Helen P., the daughter of a Danish immigrant couple, also lacked a winter coat. Unlike the outgoing Ray, Helen, red-haired and freckled, was quiet and withdrawn. No wonder! Her father paid very little attention to her, and her two brothers, tall, muscular and in their early twenties, completely ignored her. I offered to make a coat for Helen.

Hers was much more difficult to make than Ray's. The only material available was the dried-out, buffalo-hide coat, worn hairless in places, that her father had discarded years ago. I cut out the best pieces with Mrs. P.'s dull household scissors, and in doing so I developed a painfully sprained right thumb and wrist. Fortunately, Helen's uncle lent me a furrier's three-sided needle. It was sharp enough for me to poke through the tough, dried-out hide and sew the pieces together. My sprains lingered for more than a month, but Helen was warm that winter and, because I had allowed room for her to grow, for several winters to come.

Strangely enough, the only one of my three trustees (all male as usual) to complain about me during my first two years at Brightsand Lake was Helen's father. He objected to my wearing slack-type breeches when temperatures dropped as low as 40 degrees below zero Fahrenheit. He preferred a woman to wear a skirt or a dress. But Mr. P. complained only to other farmers and not to me, so I simply ignored his displeasure.

A few weeks into my third year at Brightsand Lake, however, I was unable to ignore the chairman of the school board. He was Alonzo S., a short, stocky immigrant homesteader from Tennessee, who boasted he had educated himself by studying Webster's dictionary. Years earlier he had proclaimed himself to be a biblical-type patriarch, and had established his own religious sect. He declared his children to be his "people", and vowed to beget twelve. Each Sunday he preached in the school, where he sometimes washed the feet of his "disciples".

About the middle of September 1932 the patriarch and I had a disagreement. Some of my pupils had become infected with impetigo, a highly contagious skin disease that spread rapidly throughout the school. The infectious pupils were ordered to stay at home, and the cleaning woman disinfected everything she could. Soon the impetigo epidemic seemed under control, although some home-based children, including several of the S. family, still had open sores.

Then Alonzo the patriarch announced that he would preach as usual. Apparently Mr. S., chairman of the board, had given Alonzo the patriarch permission to use the schoolroom again. The patriarch's message went forth: on the following Sunday all adults and children would be welcome.

I explained the danger of reinfection to Chairman S., but Patriarch S. refused to cancel his preaching. The other two trustees didn't care enough to intervene.

I resigned in protest. The women of the district, including Mrs. S., quickly organized an out-of-doors farewell fish fry to show their good will and to wish me luck.

With my mother's approval I spent the rest of the school year living with her in her apartment in North Battleford. For almost eight months I studied music theory, harmony, counterpoint, history and pedagogy. In mid-June I took my music exams and passed with honours.

After the exams I learned that the business school in the city would be open for one more week before closing for the summer. I attended for that week and took, at my own pace, Pitman shorthand and touch typing. I didn't continue with the shorthand, but I bought a small, portable, secondhand typewriter, and kept up my practice of touch typing. I have used that typing system ever since.

By the end of what I had expected would be my third year at Brightsand Lake, I felt that the good wishes of the women there had been amply fulfilled. I had gained much more than I had lost by resigning in protest against the authority of that unreasonable, domineering school trustee.

In September 1933 I went to my third school, my first in a town. It was at Lanigan, a small town on a main railway line in the central part of the province. The area was flat, dry and inhospitable, but I was lucky to have a job again. This time I taught only Grades 5, 6 and 7, but my salary was only half what I had earned at McLaren.

Until I went to Lanigan, my dislike of intrusive authority had nothing to do with the Royal Canadian Mounted Police. But by 1933 the depression had created widespread unemployment, poverty and hopelessness. Young unemployed men travelled the country on freight trains, hoping to find work if they travelled far enough. My background made me especially sympathetic to them.

It upset me when I learned that the resident mountie searched the boxcars lined up near the railway station, looking for illegal riders. If he found any, he either charged them with vagrancy or sent them back to the place they had just left. In my mind, the mountie I saw on the street was a well-fed, smartly uniformed disciplinarian who flushed out unkempt, hungry, unemployed men, and didn't care what happened to them. I perceived mounties as men who used their authority to maintain the painfully unfair status quo.

Unemployed women, too, suffered hardship, but they were less visible than the men. I was always lucky, perhaps because my applications to school boards stressed the value of my musical ability.

In contrast with my good fortune, many young teachers in rural Saskatchewan earned only room and board. Others were unemployed. Uneasily I thought of the bright young men I had met in North Battleford, at Normal School, and while I was teaching. Were some of them forced to ride the freights and sleep in boxcars? Probably!

In those days I believed, naively, that the federal government could have intervened to right the wrongs of Canada's heartbreaking depression. I resented the fact that the government merely set up work camps and paid men ten to twenty cents a day. And I resented the power of the mounties to force men, directly or indirectly, into those camps.

At Lanigan I came in indirect contact with a different kind of callous male authority. I learned about it one afternoon when I saw a woman huddled in a corner of the post office, weeping. She told me she was Mrs. A., and that she wept because she had no money and no hope.

Her husband had died from wounds inflicted in World War I, but she had no pension. The women for whom she used to do housework could no longer afford her. For weeks she and her children had washed in water only, because she had no money for soap. And that afternoon she had broken the handle of the axe she used to chop wood from the trees at the edge of town. She had contemplated suicide, but couldn't bear to desert her children, two of them girls in my schoolroom.

To me, the worst part of Mrs. A.'s story concerned male authority. For months she had been appealing for help from Lanigan's two churches, each of which had a finance committee of men only. The two churches were at loggerheads. Each claimed that charity was the responsibility of the other church.

I reported Mrs. A.'s plight to the chairman of my school board, a respected lawyer and a sensitive person. He gave her money for present needs, and then persuaded the town council to give her a small monthly allowance. Later my chairman arranged for her to get a war widow's pension. My contribution was to become the barber for all five A.s, so that they no longer looked as if their hair had been cut around a pudding bowl that had been turned upside down on each head.

At the end of the school year in June 1934, I decided to move on from the arid, inhospitable Lanigan, and its church-going "Christians" who hadn't tried to ease the misery of one of their townsfolk.

While spending the summer with my mother in North Battleford, I answered several school boards' newspaper advertisements. But the depression was deepening, and I received only one favourable reply. It was from the Abbey school board, and of course I went to Abbey.

Instead of achieving a more pleasant environment, as I had hoped, I found myself in the most depressed part of the province, the dust bowl. Day after day the ceaseless wind propelled balls of tumbleweed along the dusty dirt roads, and heaped them against the fences of cropless, cracked-earth fields. No one in that area seemed prosperous or hopeful.

Although I taught Grades 4, 5 and 6, I organized a school orchestra of students in the higher grades, and I stressed music in my own room. I brightened the Saturday mornings of the older girls among my pupils by letting them come to my room at the hotel where I boarded. They had a great time trying on my jewellery, especially the long drop earrings. They paraded around the room with erect posture and sparkling eyes.

As the depression worsened, it seemed as if every family in Saskatchewan were somehow affected. I felt overwhelmed by the poverty of some of the school children, especially eleven-year-old Annie who, with her younger sister, was in my classroom.

Annie was small for her age. Her appealing brown eyes seemed too large for the small face framed by lank brown hair. She wore shapeless oversized clothes, probably from one of the boxes of used clothing donated by sympathetic women in Ontario, and sent by freight trains to relief centres in the Prairie provinces.

Usually Annie and her sister drove the two miles to school in a ramshackle buggy drawn by a sway-backed horse, gray with age. If ever they failed to come to school, Annie wrote the required note of explanation because her parents, Ukrainian immigrants, couldn't write in English. One of Annie's notes explained the girls' absence thus:

> Dear Miss Hickson,
> We could not come to school last week because our horse was
> sick and we had no shoes.
> I like school.
> I like you.
> I like the perfume you gave me for my birthday. It is the best
> present I ever had.
> Your friend,
> Annie Gonolofsky

Toward the end of my school year in June 1935, soon after Annie brought me that note, many unemployed Saskatchewan men joined other unemployed westerners in the "On-To-Ottawa" trek. The trek began in British Columbia, and was moving eastward by freight train, picking up unemployed men along the way. The trekkers hoped to reach Ottawa with enough unemployed to pressure the federal government to help them.

The government, however, would have nothing to do with them. It declared that the organizers of the trek were Communists. Perhaps so, but in my view the cause was just. In any case, the RCMP, acting on government instructions, halted the trek at Regina, Saskatchewan, and ordered the trekkers to disband. So the trekkers, who included not only the young, but also middle-aged men, university graduates, an ordained minister, and a gaunt youth who sheltered a stray kitten under his threadbare sweater, returned "home". I felt even more antagonistic toward the federal government and the Mounted Police.

Meanwhile, my mother had learned that a teacher at a provincial government school near North Battleford was leaving to be married. I applied for the vacant position and was accepted. As I travelled by train from Abbey to North Battleford, where I would spend the summer with my mother, I felt safely settled at last.

To my dismay, after I had been at the provincial government school for about a year, the chairman of the board of three trustees, all male as usual, threatened to "discipline" me. He accused me of failing to notify the board in writing when I was taken critically ill after a mandatory inoculation against diphtheria. In fact, although I was almost incapacitated before I was taken to hospital, I had written to the senior teacher, asking her to notify the board. But even though the trustees knew that, and they also knew that I would be off duty for some time, the chairman reprimanded me severely, and threatened me with "punishment".

I complained to the member of the provincial legislative assembly for the North Battleford district. Soon the board of trustees was removed, and the MLA was appointed as the official trustee to represent the provincial government.

After that I had no more trouble with authoritarian school trustees, and soon my salary, paid by the provincial government, rose to what I had earned during my first teaching year, $1,000.

Nevertheless, conditions for teachers in most parts of Saskatchewan were getting worse. Salaries were falling lower and lower, and more teachers were unemployed. At one point the Saskatchewan Teachers Federation called a district meeting in North Battleford, at which we discussed going on strike. But all of us knew that there was no more money to be had, so we voted not to strike. The lucky ones among us continued to feel heartsick over the plight of the unlucky. We knew that some of our fellow teachers, like other unemployed men, were probably riding the freights and getting flushed out of boxcars by members of the RCMP.

Meanwhile a new political party, the Canadian Commonwealth Federation, had been formed in Saskatchewan in 1933. Under the leadership of M.J. Coldwell the CCF aimed at easing the distress of the unemployed and other poverty-stricken residents of the province. The following year it elected five members to the provincial legislature. Two years later, in the spring of 1936, a federal election was held, and I had my first opportunity to vote in any election.

There was little if any open support for the CCF among the hospital staff. After all, most of them were provincial Liberal appointees. Even my appointment had needed the approval of that party. The election results showed that of the approximately 150 eligible voters at the hospital, only five, including me, voted for the CCF candidate. Years later, in 1944, the CCF formed the provincial government in Saskatchewan with "Tommy" Douglas as premier, and it put into effect many of the reforms its leaders had promised, including provincially funded health care.

In the spring of 1937, however, as I lay relaxing in my basement bedroom, I didn't think consciously of any of the authoritarian males who had adversely influenced my outlook on life. Nevertheless, I was well aware that I had absolutely no desire to make friends with Constable William Kelly of the Royal Canadian Mounted Police.

Winter, 1923-24, North Battleford. Nearly 14 years old and in Grade 8. As the singing prince in King Street School's production of the musical play, "Cinderella". Costumes ordered to measure from Saskatoon.

Winter, 1924-25, North Battleford. Left, at nearly 15 years of age, as a slave girl in the professionally produced pantomime, "Aladdin and Out". I am wearing a black velveteen bolero and red silk bloomers. Costumes, as before, from Saskatoon.

Summer, 1925, Spruce Bluff. Holidaying on the farm of my Aunt Alice and Uncle Ernest Light. I am 15, and am wearing the first dress I designed and made, of pink voile. My long hair has recently been "bobbed". So has my mother's. Mine was cut by a barber, but my mother had confidently allowed me to cut hers.

1927, North Battleford. This photo in the newspaper, later called the News-Optimist, *shows me at age 17, after grade 11. I had won the gold medal for highest scholastic achievement as I did each year in high school.*

I was a teacher at age 19, and spending my McLaren school Christmas holidays with my mother.

1938, on the highway between North Battleford and Maidstone. The impoverished farmer is taking all his possessions from the dried-out dust-bowl of Southern Saskatchewan, travelling northward to find a bettter place to live.

THREE

That evening, as I sat in the living room chatting with two of the nurses who shared the apartment with me, I told them about my amusing experience in the afternoon.

"Oh, Nora!" one of them teased, "Kelly fell in love with you at first sight and didn't even notice the bumps."

"Nonsense!" I scoffed. "He didn't want to admit that his precious car was acting up!"

The next time Constable Kelly drove me home, I brought up the subject.

"Did you really think we had such a rough ride last Saturday because of the road?" I asked.

"I really did." His chuckle surprised me. Did this straight-spined mountie actually have a sense of humour? "I've just spent three years in northern Saskatchewan homestead districts," he went on. "The only roads there were narrow trails chopped through the bush."

"But surely you never had as rough a ride as we had," I persisted.

"Often," he said casually. "I usually drove a team and democrat, and we bumped over ruts, stumps and roots the whole time. During the past two and a half years, at Goodsoil, I sometimes used the little Ford roadster I had then, and often I had to stop and chop out high-rising stumps before I could drive on." He chuckled again. "I've had so much rough travel for so long that now I'm back in civilization I sometimes forget that roads are normally smooth."

No wonder this young mountie had seemed so self-reliant when the tire came off. He certainly was more mature than the other young men I knew. Even so, I didn't think any mountie was my kind of person.

Soon my mountie chauffeur and I relaxed our *American Gothic* attitudes. We became Bill and Nora, and chatted with ease. I learned that Bill had entered the baritone class of the festival. Alex Kevan, his singing teacher, would be his accompanist, but couldn't spare time for extra practice sessions. I felt sorry for Bill. As soon as I had agreed to be the choir's accompanist, Mr. Kevan had increased the number of choir practices to one on Sunday morning after church plus one, sometimes two, during the week. Considering the number of times Bill would save me inconvenient bus trips, I offered to practice with him.

"I'd be very grateful," he responded with enthusiasm.

The next evening we walked from the apartment block to my schoolroom, which housed the school piano. We went over his two festival test songs several times: the rousing "Tewksbury Road" and the plaintive love song, "I Chide Thee Not".

From the first few notes I was strongly attracted by Bill's resonant baritone. It reminded me of Nelson Eddy and Lawrence Tibbett, two of my favourite radio singers. But there was something more. Bill's voice eased an all-pervasive ache of loneliness that I had long ago accepted as normal.

"Next time you should bring some of your other songs," I suggested.

He did so. We thoroughly enjoyed Nelson Eddy songs, popular classics, and whatever else he had brought. We ended with two of the "Three Salt Water Ballads" with words by John Masefield and music by Frederick Keel. "Mother Carey" (she's the mother of the witches and all them sort o' rips) was great fun. Finally came "Trade Winds". Through the gentle wave-like rhythm and the simple but haunting strands of melody, together we evoked the call of wind, sea and far places. Like incoming warm waves rolling over a welcoming shore, contentment washed over me.

My mountie friend was my kind of person after all!

Soon Bill and I were spending most of our spare time together, at the school piano or at my mother's piano in her apartment. Then my mother invited Bill for supper one Saturday evening. He had been stationed in North Battleford too short a time to have made friends outside the Force, and he seemed to enjoy my mother's hospitality as much as my accompaniment. He pleased both of us with his polite appreciation.

As the three of us lingered at the supper table after a pleasant meal that ended with my mother's special "Queen of Puddings", she and I encouraged Bill to tell us about himself and his experiences. Immediately we could see that our dark-haired guest, with the smiling blue-gray eyes, was as eager to tell as we were to listen.

We learned that he had finished his recruit training only a few years earlier, at age twenty-three. Yet he had already spent nearly three years in sole charge at Goodsoil, the most remote of all RCMP detachments in Saskatchewan that could be reached by trail.

The Goodsoil detachment area, Bill told us, covered about 1,000 square miles of northern homesteads and Indian reservations, plus about 3,000 square miles of isolated trappers' territory of woods and lakes. All this Bill had to police from his small detachment office in the so-called "business centre" of Goodsoil. That centre contained, in addition to the RCMP detachment office, only two general stores, the Natural Resources office, a Relief Office, a log "community centre" and a blacksmith shop.

I began to admire Bill for more than his thrilling voice and his nonchalance in enduring rough roads.

"It was a tremendous territory to cover," my mother commented. "But I'd have thought there wasn't much police work to be done. After all, there weren't many people there."

"There were enough people committing crimes to keep me busy all day, every day," Bill retorted. "Then writing reports kept me busy every evening and weekend I was at home. And every time I had to escort a prisoner to jail, I had to travel about 70 miles by trail to Meadow Lake, then another 110 miles by car to North Battleford. If I was lucky, a constable from that detachment took the prisoner the rest of the way by train to the jail at Prince Albert. But no matter how long I was away from home, my work piled up and was waiting for me when I got back."

"I think I owe you an apology," Mom said.

"Not at all," Bill smiled.

Then he told us details of the work that kept him so busy. We learned that occasional thefts of grain, cattle and horses were only a small part of his work. At every season of the year he accompanied George Revell, the Natural Resources officer, on patrol, with each one lasting several days. In summer they made fish patrols, travelling in a twenty-foot Peterborough canoe equipped with an outboard motor. They advised homesteaders and part-time commercial fisherman about quotas, and about opening and closing dates of the season. Later they returned to check in case anyone was breaking the law. In the fall they made game patrols. For these they travelled with Bill's team and Revell's wagon. When the trail gave out, they unhitched the horses and rode them deep into the bush. In the winter they travelled countless miles by team and cutter or by dog sled.

When our mountie friend began telling us about his most notable case, he relived it with enthusiasm. The case concerned arson, in which three men were involved in the burning of a pool hall. Bill had charged them with conspiracy, a much more difficult offence to prove than simple arson. The accused were defended by Saskatchewan's highly reputed and very expensive criminal lawyer, John Diefenbaker, who later became Prime Minister of Canada.

Bill gave us a demonstration of Mr. Diefenbaker peering accusingly at prosecution witnesses as if they, and not his clients, were on trial. Then Mom and I watched with amusement as Bill demonstrated how Mr. Diefenbaker forcefully strode back and forth in front of the jurors, his black gown swinging and floating with each about-turn. In spite of the histrionics of their defence lawyer, however, the three arsonists were found guilty and went to jail.

My mother and I applauded Bill's performance as well as the surprising achievement of a young, inexperienced mountie. But we had a table to clear and dishes to wash.

Bill and I helped, then practiced his festival songs. Later, as he drove me home, I still glowed with admiration for my new friend. He certainly deserved a lot of credit!

The next time Bill and I enjoyed my mother's hospitality, I discovered that he deserved even more credit than I had realised. On that occasion the three of us had a light lunch at my mother's apartment after a Sunday morning church service and a festival practice. After lunch we cleared the table of Mom's best china and prettiest glasses. Then Mom and Bill did the dishes while I, by request, played pleasant background music. At last we settled ourselves comfortably, Mom and I on her gray and blue chesterfield, Bill on the maroon occasional chair. Then Mom and I again encouraged Bill to talk about his experiences.

At one point, he happened to mention that Goodsoil had no telephone.

"No telephone!" I exclaimed. "But surely there was some other way you could get advice from a senior mountie! Surely there was somebody you could contact."

"Not without a lot of trouble," Bill replied. "The nearest policeman who could advise me was Sergeant Coombs, in charge at Meadow Lake about seventy miles southeast by trail. I certainly wouldn't drive that far just to say, 'Sarge, I've got a problem.'"

"But how could you be sure that you were enforcing the law correctly?" my mother broke in. "After all, you were young and inexperienced."

"It wasn't too difficult." Bill shrugged. "I had the *Official Criminal Code*, and books on Federal and Provincial Statutes. I also had my *Constable's Manual*, which the Force issued to recruits. And I had two very useful books that I bought myself: *Crankshaw's Annotated Criminal Code* and the *Peace Officer's Manual*."

I still found it hard to believe that Bill could have policed such a huge territory alone, and with such confidence.

"Even with all those reference books," I protested, "you'd still have to trust to your own interpretation of the law. Weren't you afraid that you might sometimes be wrong? Even experienced lawyers often disagree on certain points of law."

Bill shook his head. "I always checked everything with my books the best I could," he said. "Then I did what I thought was right, and I didn't worry about it."

"It must have been difficult at times," Mom said. "Didn't any of your superiors ever disagree with you?"

Bill chuckled as he replied. Yes, sometimes the crime report reader at North Battleford sub/division disagreed with what Bill reported he had done. But crime reports with adverse criticism from a sub/division's crime readers went to the Deputy Attorney General of Saskatchewan. And he often agreed with Bill's interpretation of the law. The Deputy A.G. noted, however, that Bill's interpretation was sometimes unorthodox. In any case, the Deputy A.G.'s frequent agreement boosted Bill's self-esteem, and also his reputation.

What a remarkable young man, I thought, yet he tells these things in a matter-of-fact way, with no hint of boasting. Later I learned that some of his fellow mounties also thought him remarkable.

"I've heard so much about you, I thought you'd be a great big man," Constable Lloyd Bingham had said on meeting the twenty-six-year-old Bill in North Battleford. "Hell! You're just a kid!"

As for me, I thought that Bill's five-feet, eleven-and-a-half-inch height in his boots, and the hint of a well-muscled frame under his off-duty civilian clothes, made him just the right size.

In spite of my tendency to perceive any wrong-doer as the product of conditions beyond his control, Bill's stories made me realize that sometimes I missed relevant facts. Certainly any homesteader, no matter how impoverished, who stole another impoverished homesteader's cow, horse, grain or even chickens, was a heartless criminal who deserved to go to jail. But when our mountie friend told Mom and me about his experiences with homesteaders who made homebrew, which at first he called illicit spirits, I thought of the penniless farmers at Brightsand Lake and at Abbey, and my sympathy went out to all such people.

"I don't blame any poor homesteader for trying to make a little money from homebrew," I said. "Probably for some of them it was their only cash crop."

"Probably," Bill agreed. "But homesteaders sold their homebrew to other homesteaders who paid for it with their relief money that should have been used to buy food and clothing for their families."

"I hadn't thought of that," I said, revising my attitude.

"What's more," Bill continued, and I could see he was angry, "some of those homebrew artists put lye in their brew to give it more kick. It could blind a man or eat away his stomach. But they peddled it among their neighbours and the Indians on nearby reservations, and they didn't give a damn."

My sympathy for the homebrew makers evaporated. I didn't care what motivated them, or how poor they were. And I was glad to know that Bill cared about the Indians. They had been victimized ever since white men destroyed their way of life. I hadn't expected a Mounted Policeman to feel the way Bill evidently felt.

Long after that discussion of homebrew offences, Bill told me something that reinforced my appreciation of his attitude toward Indians. While he was still at Meadow Lake, he escorted an Indian youth to jail, using a police car. Heavy rains had turned the dirt roads to gumbo (thick, sticky mud). While Bill tried to drive the car out of deep ruts the youth, who had been pushing the car, ran away. He had gone some distance when Bill noticed him sloshing through the mud and heading for the woods. He refused to return when Bill shouted. Finally Bill fired a shot into the air, and the frightened youth returned.

Escaping custody was a serious offence that usually resulted in additional time in jail. It was Bill's duty to report the incident, and also to account for the bullet he had felt compelled to use. However, he merely completed his escort duty as usual, and didn't report the youth's attempt to escape. He obtained another bullet to add to his stock of supplies that was regularly checked by a visiting inspector, and that was the end of the matter.

"The poor kid had enough strikes against him already," Bill said sympathetically. On hearing that remark I felt a new surge of admiration for my mountie friend.

As the remaining few weeks before the music festival passed, more and more festival practices crowded my life. Somehow I made time to prepare lessons, do my laundry, wash my hair, do my nails, and so on. Most of my spare time, of course, was spent in extra practices with everyone I was accompanying, especially Bill and my mother and her friend. Sitting for hours at the piano made my chronic back problem more troublesome, but I refused to give in to it.

In the middle of April, the week of the music festival arrived. St. Paul's choir won the shield again, and so did the North Battleford Ladies' Chorus. My mother and her friend came first in their duet class, and Bill came first with his baritone solos.

My school chorus, of children aged six to ten, had no competitors, so there was nothing for us to win. But the children sang remarkably well, and I hoped for a detailed adjudication of constructive criticism. The adjudicator, however, merely scolded me sharply from the platform. My class, he snapped, sang not like children, but like professionals. Then, without another word, he strode off the platform.

I was very upset. All I had done in preparation for teaching the two obligatory songs was to explain how the children should think of the music. In well-written songs such as ours, I said, the words and the music went well together, and the most important words had a natural emphasis, especially if they came on high notes. Even young children can reason better than many adults realize, and mine responded naturally to what they understood. No matter what that carping adjudicator said, I knew that my class sang like children, but like musically aware children. I would explain to them, and we would enjoy our music together as we had always done. Even so, I still felt hurt.

On the last night of the festival, I was one of the crowd that filled Third Avenue United church. We waited patiently for the arrival of the adjudicator, who was obligated to attend the final performances and make helpful comments about the week's activities. As we waited and waited, whispers circulated that the adjudicator had been so rude to so many contestants that the festival committee had rebuked him. A fierce quarrel had ensued, and now people whispered that he was getting his own back by making us wait. At last one of the festival committee announced that we would carry on without him. Later we learned that he had stormed out of his hotel without leaving a message, and had gone home on the evening train.

I decided not to be upset another moment by the unfounded criticism of that boorish adjudicator. What did it matter that he had caused me a few hours of unhappiness during the music festival? That same festival had brought me the friendship of a young man I admired beyond words.

FOUR

A fter the festival, Bill and I sang and played for pleasure. We also had time to go to North Battleford's weekly movie. The nurses who shared the apartment were scarcely ever at home, so Bill and I had the freedom of the place. We discussed the books he bought through the Book-of-the-Month Club. I was unaware of that club, but ever since I had began earning money I had bought books. I also subscribed to *Scribners'* magazine, and together we did the *Scribners'* quizzes and enjoyed the full-page colour prints of famous paintings. I was pleasantly surprised that Bill did so well on the quizzes.

"How do you know so much about Shakespeare's plays?" I asked at one point.

He explained that as a boy he'd had elocution lessons, and had memorized some of the best-known speeches. Then in secondary school he had come first in his commercial course, and had been allowed to choose his prize. He had chosen *The Complete Shakespeare*. How remarkable! I thought.

Time seemed endless in that spring of 1937. We took leisurely walks, especially at sunset, along the south bank of the great North Saskatchewan river that bordered the hospital grounds. Together we basked in the beauty of that majestic river as it reflected the multi-coloured splendour of the northwestern sky. We saw that the vivid crimson and gold gave the lie to European art critics who pontificated that realistic Canadian paintings were no more than "cheap calendar art".

At my suggestion Bill took up golf, and we played on the nine-hole course on the hospital grounds. The course was well tended by some of the male mental patients, especially the farmers, who enjoyed the outdoor therapy and exercise.

I had learned a lot about Bill in the short time we had known each other, but golf revealed another important facet of his personality: some of his Mounted Police attitudes.

I'd had lessons from the hospital's professional golf instructor, and had played reasonably well in the hospital tournaments. The pro ordered the right clubs for Bill, as he had done for me two years earlier. I taught Bill what I had learned, and he proved to be a gifted player. Unfortunately, he was too used to being the person in charge. Soon he began telling me how to play.

"Keep your head down!" he commanded with authority again and again, just as I addressed the ball.

"Can't you see I have my head down?" I would snap back.

Bill's game improved spectacularly. Mine deteriorated, even though I tried to ignore him.

When my mountie friend knew that I often played alone, with Otto, a big, muscular, but mild-mannered patient as my caddie, he ordered me to stop using Otto. Bill, of course, knew only the dangerously disturbed patients he had escorted to the hospital. I, on the contrary, had taken, at my request, the psychiatry lectures given to the staff, so I knew about the patients. I believed that Otto was harmless, especially as the doctors allowed him to caddy as part of his therapy.

Bill always wore civilian clothes when he visited me, and when Bill asked Otto why he was in the mental hospital, he blamed "those damned mounties", who had taken him to the hospital because of a cheque he had written.

"How much was the cheque for?" Bill asked.

"About a million dollars," Otto replied.

That convinced Bill that my caddy was not a dangerous patient. Even so, my mountie friend questioned the director of the hospital about him. The director told Bill that Otto was a bachelor farmer with no close relatives. He had struggled in vain against drought, poor crops, poor grain prices, hail, and long-term debt on farm machinery. At last Otto had escaped his worries by writing worthless cheques to pay for whatever he needed. Nobody wanted the likeable bachelor to go to jail, but in those days there was no suitable institution to take care of him. So the provincial mental hospital had taken him in, but didn't confine him too strictly.

Bill still protested, but I knew that Otto's caddying meant even more to him than to me. So I used my own judgement and let him continue to caddy.

Golf also gave me a glimpse of the relationship between a junior and senior mountie.

Detective Sergeant B. was in charge of the Criminal Investigation Branch in which Bill worked. He belonged to the North Battleford Country Club, where he came first in all the tournaments. When he learned that Bill, too, was keen on golf, he invited us to play with him. After Bill accepted, he told me he admired B., not only for his golfing prowess but also for his special ability as a policeman. On the other hand, Bill warned me, Detective Sergeant B. was also coarse, ill-mannered and egotistic. Most of the constables and NCOs throughout the sub/division detested him. As soon as one of them reported an important case, B. moved in, took over, and wrote a report giving himself all the credit.

Bill overlooked B.'s faults. He explained that although B. had gone to Goodsoil as soon as he heard about Bill's arson case, and although he had assumed control of the fully prepared case, when he wrote his report, he gave due credit to Bill. Bill knew that because he routinely received a copy of B.'s report.

"I'll always remember that last sentence," Bill smiled. "It said, 'Without Constable Kelly's splendid work, this case would never have come to a satisfactory conclusion.'"

Even so, the first (and only) time we both golfed with the short, fat, strutting, cursing B., my sympathy surged to his juniors.

"How do you suppose he got into the RCMP?" I whispered to Bill as soon as were out of earshot.

"He came in automatically from the Saskatchewan Provincial Police when the Force took over Saskatchewan's provincial policing in 1928," Bill whispered back. "Just settle down and enjoy the game."

Soon I began to mistrust B.'s golf ethics. Granted, he had the skill of a professional, and his familiarity with the rough and ill-tended course gave him an advantage over Bill and me. We knew only the hospital course, well-watered and well-groomed, with velvety greens, all subsidized by the provincial government.

The Country Club course, by contrast, suffered from the general poverty of the depressed, drought-ridden 1930s. The greens weren't even green: they were big squares of sand. Before a player could putt, he had to use a long-handled wooden scraper to smooth a path from his ball to the cup. As for the fairways, they were scarcely better than the original farmland. They sprouted so many knobs of dried earth, clumps of withered grass, and scatterings of stones that players used winter rules. Thus, if a ball came to rest in a difficult position on poor terrain, the player could move it, without penalty, to a better position no closer to the hole.

What made me suspicious of the detective sergeant was that Bill and I never managed to benefit from using winter rules in the way he did. Time after time B. played along the fairway with a wooden club, whereas we always had to use irons.

"I believe he cheats!" I said angrily to Bill as we approached the fifth hole with difficulty, while B. strode far along the sixth fairway.

"If he does, it's his problem," Bill shrugged.

During the rest of the game I paid more attention to B. than to my own game. I saw that if Bill and I were not too near when B. repositioned his ball, he surreptitiously tapped in place the top half of a broken tee he had taken from his pocket. Then he casually placed his ball on the scarcely visible tee, used a driver or a spoon to lift it an amazing distance, and swaggered after it.

"We should let him know we know," I said to Bill on the way home. "He probably uses the same system to win at tournaments."

"Don't be stupid!" Bill admonished me. "I could never accuse a detective sergeant of cheating! He'd get back at me somehow!"

"At least we should stop playing with him," I persisted.

Bill, however, felt he couldn't afford to offend B. He still played occasionally with him, although I never did.

Three years later, Bill and I were living in Toronto. Walking along Yonge Street one bright Sunday afternoon, we came to a sporting goods store with an open box of tees in the window.

"We should send a box to B., in memory of our games with him," Bill suggested.

"Humph!" I retorted. "It would be more suitable to break the tees in two, and send him only the top halves!"

We did so, but without putting a return address on the package, so we never heard if B. actually received it.

We did hear of him again, though, many years later. Meanwhile, Bill's former Officer Commanding at North Battleford, Inspector Frank Spriggs, had become Superintendent Spriggs and had retired. Bill by then had become an inspector, so the difference in rank of the two men no longer mattered. When Superintendent and Mrs. Spriggs visited Halifax, where Bill and I were stationed, we were as hospitable as possible. Bill and the superintendent reminisced, and I felt free to ask about Detective Sergeant B.

"I always mistrusted him," I said, "but Bill always defended him."

Bill mentioned his arson case, which he knew Spriggs would remember as it was a successful conspiracy case. Bill stressed that in the last sentence of B.'s report on the arson case, he had acknowledged Bill's splendid work.

"Don't give B. any credit for that," Spriggs said curtly. "He turned in his report with no mention of you, Kelly. I ordered him to correct it, giving you the credit you deserved. So B. added that last sentence."

I thought of the box of broken tees, and hoped that B.'s remarkable detective ability had enabled him to deduce who had sent it.

1934, Regina. Bill standing outside his barrack room. He has just passed his recruit training exams and has been issued with his first red serge.

1936, North Battleford. Photo taken while I was teaching at the Provincial Mental Hospital school.

Summer, 1937, North Battleford. Bill on the golf course at the Provincial Mental Hospital.

FIVE

During the post-festival month of June 1937 I learned a lot more about Bill. The friendly nurses who shared the apartment now took it for granted that Bill and I would use the place as we liked. Our frequent and prolonged talk sessions brought out the fact that Bill's father, a miner in Wales, had brought his family to Canada for the same reason my mother had brought me – for more opportunity than would otherwise have been available.

I learned that Mr. Kelly had bought a farm in New Brunswick where he hoped to make a good living growing potatoes. But the soil was poor, fertilizer was expensive, and potato prices were as low as ten cents a barrel. So Bill, recently turned seventeen, worked to pay the expenses on the farm. He worked in a mine, on a St. John river freighter, in a lumber camp, on the railroad laying ties and on a dairy farm. At last he found security by joining the RCMP. Later his father was plagued by serious illness. Mr. and Mrs. Kelly and their three younger children returned to Great Britain, glad that Bill, at least, had been lucky.

I also learned that even before the Kellys left Wales, Bill had helped with the family finances. He had gathered food for the pig his family raised each year, and after the pig was butchered, Bill was the one who went to relatives and friends, taking orders for the choicest cuts of meat. Later he delivered the meat and collected the money for it.

With his mother's encouragement, but on his own initiative,

teenaged Bill had organized a "Christmas chocolate club". He took orders for boxes of chocolates, collected small weekly instalment payments, ordered the chocolates from a company in England, and delivered them in time for Christmas. For this he earned a commission plus boxes of chocolates, which he sold for extra money. He also sold and delivered eggs on commission from a commercial chicken farm. He took orders from miners' families and the town's hospital, sometimes as many as sixty dozen weekly.

On learning about Bill's early aggressive salesmanship, I admired him more than ever. I, too, had earned money when I was young, but I would never have had the confidence to push out on my own as he had done.

When I was fourteen I worked on Saturdays, at first in Woolworth's at twenty cents an hour, and then in a dry goods store at a slightly higher rate. But I hadn't even needed to apply for those jobs: someone else had got them for me. Neither did it take any courage to enter my hand-sewing and India ink maps in contests at the annual agricultural fair, where I always won cash prizes. When I was fifteen, I didn't apply for the job of playing the piano for the Continuing Presbyterians: they offered it to me. I also earned money by playing, on request, for a dance class, for dancing at young people's parties, and occasionally at Saturday afternoon teas given by well-to-do ladies. The teas provided a higher rate of pay, but earning it was less satisfying. Nobody paid any attention to the music, but the fee-paying hostess was satisfied if it encouraged conversation.

During one week of the summer I was fifteen, I substituted, also by request, for the woman who played the piano at the silent movies in the city's only theatre. The sheet music that came with the reels of film – Beethoven's *Sonata Pathetique*, for example – was much too difficult for me to sight read. So I simply looked up at the screen and played something suitable as the images flickered past. What I enjoyed most was improvising exciting and noisy music when the cowboy hero was being chased over the cactus-dotted badlands by the villain's gun-toting gang.

For playing at two consecutive shows, on each of six evenings, plus one Saturday matinee, I earned five dollars. That was good pay in those days, equal to more than twenty times that amount in today's currency, about three-quarters of a century later.

On the way home on Saturday night I found that the city's jewellery establishment, which also sold a few pieces of fine china, was still open. I went in and bought a gift for my mother. For weeks I had seen it in the jeweller's window, and had longed to buy the lovely streamlined azure-blue teapot, tastefully decorated in silver and somehow reminding me of Aladdin's lamp. But it was expensive, and I couldn't afford it. Now, however, I was rich enough to buy it. By the time I got home with my precious package it was about midnight, but my mother was still up, waiting for me. She was delighted with the gift. My week's earnings had brought me the satisfaction of my mother's pleasure at receiving the beautiful teapot, plus one dollar and five cents change from my five-dollar bill.

I didn't tell Bill about my youthful earnings at the time he told me about his. In fact, my achievement seemed much less than his. I was very conscious of the fact that I'd always had jobs offered to me. Bill, on the other hand, had pushed his way toward earning money. I marvelled at his strength of purpose. What a remarkable person he was!

By the end of my teaching year in June 1937 Bill and I had known each other only a little more than three months, but we seemed like two halves of one whole. Even so, neither of us seemed to realize that perhaps we were in love.

With the approach of July 1, however, when I was due to leave on a long-planned, two-month holiday with my mother, I ached to stay in North Battleford, near Bill. On the other hand, I couldn't disappoint my mother. Now that I was teaching near home, I was trying to repay my debt to her with what she seemed to value most – my company.

The previous summer, the first in which I could afford an expensive trip, which also happened to be the year of Vancouver's jubilee celebrations, my mother and I had holidayed in that city. For two wonderful months we two drought and depression creatures had revelled in flowers, fountains, parks, Emily Carr evergreens, the ocean, and operas and Shakespearean plays staged outdoors in Stanley Park. We had promised ourselves a second holiday in Vancouver the following summer. Now that summer had arrived, but I didn't want to leave Bill!

Still, I must consider all the advantages my mother had given me, many of which had been through the sacrifice of her own welfare. There was so much: emigrating to Canada, shielding me from the harsh conditions of our first three years here, a piano, *Books of Knowledge*, music lessons, dancing lessons, even pretty blouses she made by hand before she could afford a sewing machine. All had been for my benefit. And the amazing thing, to me, about those precious gifts was that my mother had given them without love, or at least without any overt signs of love.

Although my memory went back to the time I was six months old, a baby in my carriage, I remembered only one brief moment of a physical demonstration of maternal love. Granted, I always had a perfunctory kiss on the cheek at bedtime, but that didn't seem to count.

Only one incident had impressed me: my only conscious memory of my mother's warm embrace. The memory went back to a Saturday afternoon in November 1918, about the time of the armistice that ended World War I. I was eight then, at home in bed, critically ill with the "soldiers disease" of trench mouth and the deadly Spanish flu. During the week, when my mother was teaching, she left me with a hand mirror so that I could reflect sunlight here and there on walls and ceiling, and so have "Joe Bush" for company till she came home at noon and after school. But this was Saturday, so she was there to look after me.

My memory begins with her seated on the edge of the bed, holding a spoonful of castor oil and trying to persuade me to take it. When at last I swallowed the revolting oil, she threw her arms about me and held me tight in that memorable embrace. I learned later that she had expected me to die. At the time, the unfamiliar sensation of my mother's arms about me was so strange that the embrace seemed not to belong to me. Nevertheless, even now, about eighty years later, the sensation lingers undiminished.

During the three years my mother was my teacher at one-room schools at Brightsand Lake and Spruce Bluff, she was more strict with me than with anyone else. She took off many marks for small errors she ignored in other pupils' work.

Once, when the two oldest boys in the school (Helen P.'s older brothers) misbehaved in the schoolyard at recess, my mother knew she must assert her authority or lose control. She decided to strap not only the offending boys but also some of the other children who had stood and watched. This presumably would put the fear of the strap into all the pupils. She chose the watching offenders by age, and included me but no one younger. I was ten, and considered I had done nothing wrong. The heartache I felt, as much as the sting of the leather strap on my sensitive palm, reinforced my sense of being unloved.

When we moved to North Battleford and I had other teachers, I came first in my class each year to the end of high school. Yet even 100 per cents didn't elicit one word of praise or even acknowledgement, neither did my taking the lead each year in the annual high-school play, nor even my progress in music. In fact I was so used to my achievements being ignored that when, at the end of my last year in high school, the IODE (Independent Order of the Daughters of the Empire) offered me a scholarship to help me through university, I didn't tell my mother of the offer either then or later. Instead, I politely refused it, explaining that I must begin to earn my own living, which in reality I longed to do.

My mother's lack of approval was especially hurtful. At first, long before I could translate my feelings into words, I regarded her as omnipotent. As I grew older I recognized her as the cleverest, strongest, most competent person I knew. Her lack of approval made me believe that, for some reason unknown to me, I must be unworthy of praise, and hence inferior and unworthy of love.

When I grew old enough to consider such matters I found it strange that my mother had been so generous and so self-sacrificing. The only explanation seemed to be that since she hadn't done so much for love, she must have done it from a sense of duty. Therefore I in turn had a duty to do whatever I could for her. And as I grew older, my sense of obligation grew stronger.

After experiencing more than half a century of believing myself unloved, I became anxious to sort out my memories. I asked my mother why she had always been more strict with me than with anyone else. She explained that she had always done it on purpose. She had feared that otherwise both teachers and pupils would have accused her of favouring me. It was a welcome revelation, but my feelings of being unloved and unworthy had been with me too long. I never quite overcame my sense of inferiority.

With the approach of July 1, 1937, I had a strong sense of obligation to keep my promise to take a second summer holiday in Vancouver. Although I ached to stay near Bill, I must go with Mom. I also had an obligation to Mr. and Mrs. Kevan. Mom and I had arranged to go to the coast with them, travelling in their car and sharing expenses.

There was a third reason, equally valid, that I should take my holiday as planned. I had been taught, as were most young women in those days, that it was improper to make advances to a young man. So it seemed highly inadvisable that I should forego a long-planned holiday to stay near a young man who hadn't even asked me not to go. No! Rather than reveal my longing to be near Bill, I would endure two miserable months in alien Vancouver. My pride would force me to conceal my unhappiness.

Bill and I promised to write to each other, and I packed writing materials and stamps, planning to use them the moment we arrived. As it happened, I wrote my first letter to Bill when we had gone only about twenty miles.

At that point Mr. Kevan's car broke down. Mrs. Kevan, my mother and I stood uncomfortably or wandered aimlessly while Mr.

Kevan prowled the village until he found a garage mechanic who agreed to fix the car even though it was July 1, the national holiday, Dominion Day. I spent part of my time sitting on a big rock, writing to Bill about the mishap. The rest of the time I spent trying in vain to think of a logical and acceptable reason that I should go home on the train that would pass through the village that evening, on the way to North Battleford and Bill.

After that I wrote to Bill from wherever we stayed for the night. There were plenty of things to report. In those days tourist cabins were scarce and ill-equipped. We carried our bedding with us, and made do with only cold water for washing and showering. We visited caves and, in the United States, the site of the huge Grand Coulee Dam. It was then under construction among hills whose sides were frozen to prevent their collapse.

The mountains were spectacular, but as we began travelling through them, Mom and I noticed with alarm that for much of the time Mr. Kevan failed to keep to his own side of the road. He always avoided the outer edge of the narrow, winding roads, which in those days had no dividing lines. Neither did they usually have protective fences, even where the road curved dangerously near the edge of a deep chasm. It was impossible to see far ahead, and Mom and I, in the back seat, whispered our fears that an oncoming car would crash into us as we travelled around curves on the side of the road intended for oncoming traffic. Fortunately there wasn't much traffic in those days, but after the third near miss my nerves gave way.

I leaned forward and shouted hysterically into Mr. Kevan's ear. "Why don't you keep to your own side of the road!"

He pulled into the next lookout area. We all got out and had drinks of tea from our thermos flasks, trying to pretend that nothing had happened. But my mother and I were visibly shaken, and Mr. Kevan looked even more distraught.

"Alex's trouble," Mrs. Kevan explained soothingly, "is that he's afraid of heights. Whenever our side of the road is too near the edge of a deep drop, he's afraid we'll fall in. So he drives over to the other side, where there is only a towering cliff, and he feels safe."

She promised that in future Alex would keep to his own side of the road, but apparently he couldn't. When at last we reached Vancouver, Mom and I were thankful we had arranged to go home by train.

Just as I had anticipated, Vancouver in the summer of 1937 failed to interest me. Flowers, trees, fountains, and even the ocean, all seemed insubstantial. Friends, relations, and even my mother seemed scarcely to exist. My real world centred on my letters to Bill and his to me.

I made mine as bright and amusing as possible, and short enough that Bill wouldn't lose interest. His to me reported almost everything he had done. He stuffed his numerous pages into whatever lay near at hand, usually long brown envelopes marked RCMP.

"You'll have difficulty sleeping with this one under your pillow," my mother teased me one day as she saw me open the two RCMP envelopes that held Bill's latest report. It was the longest and bulkiest to date, and had of necessity been mailed in two sections.

Nevertheless, I tucked all twenty-four pages under my pillow that night, just as I tucked each letter in turn during the whole holiday.

At the risk of flouting the proprieties firmly established by the women's magazines of that period, I sent Bill a gift, a little box of six marzipan piglets, meant to remind him of the newborn piglets we had seen when we toured the hospital farm buildings. Also, I bought him some songs made popular by his two favourite baritones, Lawrence Tibbett and Nelson Eddy. But I was determined not to seem to be enticing him with gifts. I decided to pretend that I had bought "Short'nin' Bread", "The Donkey Serenade" and "The Green-eyed Dragon" for my own pleasure in their showy accompaniments.

On the heart-warming evening in late August when my mother and I arrived home by train, Bill was there to meet us. After a light supper with Mom, Bill drove me home to the hospital. Sitting beside him in that familiar Ford coupé, travelling over the familiar gravelled highway, I glowed with happiness. Bill seemed happy, too, as we picked up the threads of communication precisely where our letters had left off. We still babbled contentedly as he carried my suitcase down into my basement room and swung it up on the bed for ease of unpacking.

Then he turned and looked at me as if to savour the fact that I really had come back. Suddenly I found myself in his arms.

"I didn't want you to go," he murmured.

"Neither did I," I confessed.

Talk was no longer necessary, and pretence would have been ridiculous. As for the proprieties, from that moment, they might as well never have existed.

Summer, 1936, Vancouver. Snapshot of me in Stanley Park was taken, at her suggestion, by my mother.

Summer, 1936, Vancouver. On rocky shore of Stanley Park while holidaying with my mother.

1936, Vancouver. Taking time out from tennis in Stanley Park.

Summer, 1937, in the Rocky Mountains. Snapshot taken while my mother and I travelled through the Rockies by car with Mr. and Mrs. Alex Keven, en route to the west coast.

SIX

The first three weeks of September radiated happiness. I'd never loved anyone before, although I'd had boyfriends. As for Bill, he'd never had time for girls before he joined the RCMP. Then he had immersed himself in his studies, and later in his fascinating work. Now Bill, 26, and I, 27, experienced the overwhelming magnetism of first love. Without inhibitions we flung ourselves into the delights, physical and mental, of that amazing attraction. Every weekend and every evening, except when Bill was on duty, we spent together. And I naively basked in a sense of permanence, as if the joys of living and loving would continue, unabated and without interruption, forever.

On Monday, September 20, the RCMP shattered my illusions.

"I've been transferred to Maidstone!" Bill exclaimed with enthusiasm the moment he arrived at my apartment that evening. "It's only for three months, relieving Corporal Len Hobbs while he's in Regina on a refresher course. But it means the OC trusts me with a detachment that rates a corporal."

His next news was even more shocking. He was to leave the next day! I felt almost panicky as I realized how easily the Mounted Police could transfer Bill right out of my life. Then there was more bad news. Although Maidstone was only sixty miles from North Battleford, the boundary of the detachment area fell short of North Battleford by twenty-five miles. Bill would be the only mountie in the whole area, and unless he had to escort a prisoner or a mental patient, he wouldn't be allowed to leave it.

"Don't look so glum," Bill said. "You know the Force transfers unmarried men at short notice whenever it's necessary. They don't want the expense of moving married men with families and furniture. Cheer up!"

"I'm glad your OC has confidence in you," I said, trying to be sensible. "As for me, I'll spend the next three months concentrating on my school work. I've been neglecting it lately."

"It won't be as bad as that," Bill said soothingly. He put his arms around me. "You can come to visit me on weekends. You can come by train and stay at the hotel."

I hesitated. I didn't mind ignoring the proprieties in private, but how could I shamelessly pursue this attractive young mountie in public? I'd feel like a camp follower, and that's how other people would regard me, too. On the other hand, why should I let the RCMP control my life as completely as it did Bill's?

"I don't like the idea of traipsing after you," I protested, "but I'll come for a weekend after you're well settled. Train service between here and Maidstone is good."

Mail service was good, too. First-class mail going between communities on main railway lines was quick and reliable, all for the price of a three-cent stamp on each letter. In fact, mail was sorted en route by mail clerks travelling on the trains.

Bill's letter of Friday, September 24, which I received on Saturday, told me that Corporal Hobbs had left that morning, and Bill was working hard to get settled. His Saturday letter, received Monday noon, announced that he was well settled, so I could come any weekend.

His Sunday letter, received Monday after school, announced that when I went I wouldn't have to stay at the hotel. Mrs. Hobbs, remaining at the police house with her three-year-old daughter, had noticed Bill moping. She had invited me to stay with her, as soon and as long as I liked.

"You won't have to travel by train, either," Bill's letter continued. "I can make a highway patrol to the eastern boundary of my detachment area any Friday night. Then I'll sneak into North Battleford and pick you up. On Sunday night I'll patrol again, and drive you home. How about coming this Friday, darling?"

"Sorry," I wrote regretfully by return mail. "I need this weekend to catch up on my school work."

On Friday night I went to bed as usual, and soon drifted into the sound sleep of one who has done her duty by staying at home. About midnight I was awakened by someone shaking my shoulder. There was Bill, in breeches, boots and brown serge workday tunic. We didn't lock the doors in our apartment building because the nurses constantly went in and out of one another's suites. Bill had simply walked in.

"Hurry up and get dressed," he said, bending to kiss me. "I've got to get back to my own district before anybody sees me."

Drowsily I donned my day clothes and fumbled to find a few necessities to put into a small suitcase.

"Hurry up!" Bill kept on saying. "Can't you move any faster?"

Sleepily I dragged myself after him, out to the police car, unmarked as was usual then. Soon the chill of the night air dispelled my lethargy. Alert and smugly content that apparently we didn't always have to do exactly as the Mounted Police said, I snuggled down beside my wayward mountie. It didn't disturb me that he broke the speed limit as we sped along the gravel highway and headed for Maidstone.

The moment we reached Bill's detachment area, he slowed the car and prepared to resume his highway patrol duties. They were not onerous, since there were only a few vehicles on the road at that time of night. Bill simply had to stop every oncoming car or truck, check each driver's license, and warn any "one-eyed" driver to get his ailing light fixed. On rare occasions he would also have to apprehend a known wanted criminal who was surreptitiously travelling by night.

Of course it was absolutely against rules and regulations that I was travelling in a police car. As I saw the first headlights coming toward us from the distant horizon of the flat, straight highway, I suddenly felt alarmed. But I had no time to express my fears.

"Climb into the back!" Bill ordered sharply. "Lie on the floor and hide under the blanket till I tell you it's safe to come out!"

In those days women rarely wore slacks. So I was wearing a dress and my brown bouclé form-fitting fall coat that had big lapels covered with sleek brown fur (rabbit, of course, this time masquerading as seal). The coat also had a wide brown leather belt that set off my trim waist, but made the coat even less practical for climbing. I was also wearing a hat, a smart one-sided beige felt. And until Bill shouted at me, I had been sitting decorously, holding my brown leather clutch bag in my gloved hands. Nevertheless, like a well-trained hound obeying its master's command, I threw my bag and hat into the back seat and sprang after them. On the floor of that police car I crouched, with my hat and bag, under the heavy, scratchy gray blanket that I learned later was a police-issue from Bill's police bed.

At the opportune moment, Bill stopped the car and got out. His breeches, boots, tunic and stetson, silhouetted in the glare of the police car lights behind him, typified authority. He waved the oncoming car to a stop, and checked whatever seemed necessary. After allowing the driver to move on, he got back in the police car and continued his night patrol.

"All clear!" he called to me when there was no longer any danger of my being seen.

I clambered back into the front seat, fine-tuned and alert, minus my hat and bag, ready to spring again into the back of the two-door Ford sedan the moment the next headlights gleamed on the horizon. Fortunately for me, none of the checked vehicles held a wanted criminal. Otherwise I'd have had to travel the rest of the way to Maidstone huddled under the scratchy blanket on the floor of the back seat, while the criminal sat comfortably in front with Bill.

We pulled in at the Maidstone detachment about two o'clock in the morning, and tiptoed into the big two-story house rented by the police. Bill tapped gently on the door of Mrs. Hobbs' main-floor bedroom. A few moments later a sleepy, pretty blonde young woman emerged and invited me to share her bed. Bill went out to the separate little office, where he slept soundly under "my" rough gray blanket.

SEVEN

On Saturday morning, while Bill worked in his office, Tena and I sat at her kitchen table drinking tea. Pretty little Peggy, blonde and dainty like her mother, sat playing on a blanket spread over the linoleum-covered kitchen floor.

"Welcome to Mounted Police life," Tena said, "although I don't recommend it."

I soon understood her attitude. She and Len had met and fallen in love when they both worked in the north. She was a nurse, he a corporal in the RCMP. Before marriage they both enjoyed their northern service. But after Tena gave up nursing, and she and Len were married, Tena was overwhelmed with work expected of her simply because she was the wife of a Mounted Policeman.

In spite of her reluctance she had been drawn into mothering several unmarried constables, even to baking their bread and darning their socks. Whenever the police had a prisoner, she cooked his meals. Even after baby Peggy was born, Tena was expected to work ceaselessly.

"Didn't Len help you?" I asked in surprise.

"Oh, yes," Tena replied, "and so did the others – when they were home. But sometimes all the men were away on long patrols for weeks at a time. Then, as well as looking after myself and my baby, I had to melt snow, carry water, stoke fires and carry out ashes. The last straw was having to attend to visiting missionaries, Indians and Eskimos. They all expected to be treated the same way as when Len was at home, and of course I couldn't insult them."

"That's shocking!" I sympathized, feeling pity for the slight young woman who seemed too fragile to have been forced to endure such hardships. "You must have been thankful when you were transferred to Maidstone."

That transfer, however, meant that Tena had merely traded old problems for new ones. The Hobbs family had scarcely settled in when Len was sent on the three-month refresher course. So Tena, still not fully recovered from the rigours of the north, had to remain in Maidstone, without supportive friends, and with full responsibility for herself and her little daughter. No wonder her blue eyes were sometimes clouded with unhappiness! No wonder she looked so harrassed!

"Now you know why I don't recommend Mounted Police life." She smiled ruefully.

"Indeed I do," I replied somberly.

Later that morning Bill took me out to see his office. It seemed as unappealing as Tena's existence. It occupied most of the square, shed-like frame building in which the rough floor reeked of cedar oil. Its only furnishings were a desk, a small table holding a typewriter, three plain wooden chairs, some filing cabinets and a cast-iron, pot-bellied heater. To the left of the entrance stood the steel-barred cell with a steel cot.

Bill's bedroom flanked the end wall of the cell. The room, box-like and windowless, was scarcely big enough to hold the narrow bed with its white enamelled bedstead, a kitchen chair, a rough wooden washstand, and Bill's upright wardrobe trunk. The trunk stood open and unpacked because he had nowhere better to put his clothes.

"It's much worse here than at Goodsoil," Bill said apologetically. "But it's not the fault of the Force," he continued loyally. "The federal government pays the rent for police premises, and patronage to local politicians determines who rents to the police."

After lunch at the local hotel I spent the afternoon with Tena. As Bill explained, Saturday was his busiest day because most farmers came to town on Saturday. Men continuously came to the detachment to make complaints about theft or trespass, or to report to Bill as he had ordered them to do. I had to spend Saturday night with Tena, too. There were more vehicles on the highway than at any other time, so Bill had to patrol it.

However, we were together for meals, and for a few hours after Bill's night patrol. ("Make good use of the chesterfield," Tena had said with a knowing smile, so we did.) We were also together on Sunday, and for the return drive to North Battleford on Sunday night, when I occasionally had to spring to the floor of the back seat as I had done during our Friday night patrol. In any case, it was satisfying to have outwitted the autocratic RCMP.

Over the next few weekends our regular Friday and Sunday night drives gave me unique pleasure. Looking out at the myriad stars shining through the clear, unpolluted air, I was keenly aware of what infinitesimal specks we humans are by comparison with the immense mass of any star. It was comforting to remember that we, too, are worthy components of the universe.

Sometimes the harvest moon hung low in the sky, looking like an oversized replica of itself at other seasons. Its soft glow created surprisingly sharp shadows of the leafless bushes and trees that edged the highway. The bewitching beauty of those harvest-season drives under the great star-filled sky dome filled me with awe. Most amazing, however, was that I also had Bill. I was the luckiest of mortals!

After my first weekend at Maidstone I took books to read, exercise notebooks to mark, and lesson materials to organize. As Bill and I grew bolder, I did some of my work sprawled on his bed, seeing by the light of the window he'd had a carpenter install. Meanwhile, Bill did his work in the outer office.

Often at night we snuggled close together on his hard, narrow police bed, letting our favourite radio programs shield us from the ugliness of our surroundings. Sometimes, too, I coaxed Bill to tell me more of his fascinating experiences. I heard about the time he took Saskatchewan's quinquennial census in his vast area of inaccessible lakes and forests. He flew in a two-seater plane equipped with pontoons, hired from Prince Albert along with a bush pilot who flew "by the seat of his pants". They touched down on the edge of lakes that reflected the azure of the cloudless sky in water as smooth as the liquid in a drinking glass. Isolated trappers and fishermen and their families hurried out to greet them, and Bill took the census. I thought back to my childhood reading of the *Arabian Nights*, and found the two-seater plane as adventursome as the flying carpet. What fascinating experiences Bill had had!

I also heard stories of his bitterly cold winters. The Goodsoil detachment had no thermometer, and one sunlit morning he drove in his little Ford roadster to make an investigation in a distant village. When he arrived, he learned that the blacksmith's outdoor thermometer had frozen, indicating that the temperature was probably about seventy degrees below zero Farenheit. Even so, Bill disregarded the fact that his car might break down in the unsettled wilderness, and drove back to Goodsoil and work.

I considered telling Bill about my own experiences with winter cold, but decided against it. Granted, during one year when I taught at Brightsand Lake I lived in a granary. It had only a small heater, and winter temperatures dropped as low as forty degrees below zero Farenheit. But the granary had been scrubbed clean and white-washed, and it sat in the yard of a farmer whose wife provided my meals and school lunches. She also provided me with a feather bed and a feather comforter to keep me warm at night. And each morning before she called me to get up for breakfast, she tiptoed in and lit a roaring fire in my little heater, and brought me hot water for washing. Obviously my winter hardships couldn't compete with Bill's.

His story of one winter patrol made me shiver, not from thoughts of cold, but from imagining a fatal outcome. He had driven with a team and cutter down the length of a frozen lake to the cabin of a trapper. After Bill and his team left for home, the trapper, by mistake, let his two half-wolf dogs out of the shed where he had put them when Bill arrived. My mountie love had been chased by those two vicious, frenzied animals as he drove back over the frozen lake. They had raced near enough to snatch off the cutter's buffalo robe, but had paused to tear it apart before continuing their attack. At last Bill was forced to shoot one of them. The other dog paused to savage the dead one, and Bill and his frothing, steaming team escaped. I trembled to think of what might have happened, and I held Bill close in thanksgiving.

When I stayed too late with Bill, and had to go to the outdoor toilet, Bill stood guard at the office door, ready to warn me of any passersby. We knew he could have been severely disciplined, probably dismissed, for having me in the detachment office. Nevertheless, we merely took care not to let anyone but Tena know what we were doing. The three of us joyfully celebrated our conspiracy while consuming Bill's purchases of marshmallows for our coffee, mushrooms for weekend treats, and oversized boxes of maraschino cherry chocolates.

Bill and I were not formally engaged when I first went to Maidstone. In fact, he never did propose. He seemed to take it for granted that we'd marry as soon as possible. I had been of the same mind until I heard Tena's shocking stories.

One Saturday night, after Bill's highway patrol and after Tena had gone to bed, we were sitting on her chesterfield, making plans for the next day. Suddenly Bill changed the subject.

"I have to tell you about the Force's marriage regulations," he said seriously. "I have to serve six years before I can get permission to marry. That means we'll have to wait till July 6, 1939."

"What a domineering organization you belong to!" I exclaimed, moving to the far end of the chesterfield. "Your Force has a lot of nerve, making you serve six years and then making you ask permission to marry! It's even worse than Tena told me!"

"Anyway, that's how it is," Bill said philosophically. "What kind of engagement ring would you like?"

"I don't want an engagement ring," I said firmly. "I love you very much, but I don't want to get involved with your precious Force. And I specially don't want to end up like Tena."

"Don't be like that," Bill said soothingly. He slid along to my end of the chesterfield and put an arm around my shoulders. "You'd never have Tena's kind of problems. Only volunteers go north, and I'd never volunteer."

"I don't want to get moved about the way you do, either," I said. "Your six or seven different postings in three years don't appeal to me. I've never been settled anywhere for long, and when I get married I want to settle down."

"You'd never had to worry about that, either," Bill said gently. "You know it's only because I'm single that I've been moved so often." He put his hand on my head, and guided it down to his shoulder. "Just relax, and I'll tell you what our life will be like after we're married."

According to Bill, it would be blissful. We'd stay in Saskatchewan, where he had first served, the way it usually happened. We'd share an idyllic life in a pleasant little town. Bill would be in charge of a well-cared-for detachment with the office next to the house, or perhaps even in the house. After breakfast he would have to go to his office, of course, but he'd step into "my" kitchen for a cup of midmorning coffee and a hug. He'd come home again for lunch, for afternoon tea and, of course, for supper. We'd be together most of the time, perfectly happy.

"It sounds wonderful," I said. "But I don't want an engagement ring."

I still was reluctant to be permanently associated with the highly disciplined RCMP and its short-notice transfers and refresher courses. Furthermore, I found it demeaning that wives were regarded merely as useful adjuncts whether they liked it or not. Also, I knew that if conditions as a mountie's wife became unbearable, I wouldn't be able to escape: my love for Bill would shackle me to the Force. Nevertheless, Bill's persuasive description of my life as a mountie's wife eventually overcame my caution.

"I would like a ring," I admitted one night. "I'd like one just like

Tena's."

"That's wonderful!" Bill beamed, hugging me tight. "Unfortunately, you'll have to wait till I can leave my detachment area and get to a suitable jeweller."

At last he had to escort a prisoner to Prince Albert, where there was not only a jail, but also a "suitable jeweller". Bill had to return to Maidstone by way of North Battleford, so he paid me a surprise visit and presented me with a ring exactly like Tena's. It was white gold, with a central diamond flanked by two smaller ones. Moreover, it was a perfect fit.

The next weekend, at Maidstone, Tena ignored the hardships she had warned me against, and shared in our happiness. When she and I went to do her grocery shopping, of course I wore my engagement ring, and she insisted that I "show and tell" everyone we met.

So now I was officially engaged, and looking forward to the idyllic married life that Bill had so persuasively foretold.

Fall, 1937, Maidstone. Bill and I are leaning against the detachment police car. I am wearing the brown bouclé coat in which I made my first night patrol.

1937, Maidstone. While I was visiting Tena Hobbs, Bill took this snap of me with the dog, Gyp, owned by Inspector Frank Spriggs, but cared for by Tena.

Tena's Peggy

EIGHT

A few weeks later, Bill's OC, Inspector Frank Spriggs, inspected the Maidstone detachment. At lunchtime he and Bill, both in uniform, strode smartly in step along the wooden sidewalk toward the hotel. The faint jingle of their spurs, no longer suitable for use in the mechanized 1930s, attested to the Force's link with tradition.

Suddenly the inspector took his swagger stick from under his arm and tapped Bill's nearest boot with it.

"Police cars are for police business, young fellow," he said sharply, without breaking step.

"Yes sir!" Bill agreed firmly, also without breaking step. And that was the end of the conversation.

It was also the end of my night patrols. After that I went to Maidstone by train. I left North Battleford about nine o'clock on Friday evening and arrived at Maidstone about eleven. On Monday morning I had to leave Tena's bed about half past five to reach North Battleford about eight o'clock. I had breakfast at the Dominion (Chinese) cafe, where the mounties usually ate. There Dick Kwan, a likeable young Chinese waiter, had my breakfast set out. After breakfast I took a three-mile, fifty-cent taxi ride to the hospital, arriving in plenty of time to change my clothes and ring the school handbell at nine o'clock.

Eventually Bill learned that a North Battleford constable on night patrol had reported seeing us. But we were lucky. Although Inspector

Spriggs could have formally charged Bill with several serious offences, we heard no more on the subject.

We were lucky, too, that Corporal Hobbs' refresher course ended before Christmas. So Bill and I spent the festive season with my mother, who always gave us her blessing no matter how we flouted the proprieties.

With Bill stationed in North Battleford again, early in the new year we began preparing for the 1938 music festival in North Battleford. If Bill won there, he was entitled to enter the Northern Provincial Festival in Saskatoon. If he won there, he could enter the Northern finals, also in Saskatoon, singing his own choice. Ambitiously we began working on the *Prologue* from *Pagliacci*. Difficulties arose immediately. Bill didn't read music fluently, and the music went through numerous changes of key, tempo, mood and so on. But I had faith, and we persevered.

About the middle of February, the RCMP did it again! Bill was ordered to Cutknife immediately, to relieve Constable Bert Torrens, who had accumulated a month's leave, and had permission to marry. I thought that the Force's use of Bill, so soon after his Maidstone duty, was most unfair. Bill, however, accepted it as normal.

The small town of Cutknife was only thirty miles west of North Battleford, but it might as well have been three hundred. As at Maidstone, Bill couldn't leave his detachment area, but in any case the roads were so clogged with snow at that time of year that cars couldn't operate. Trains went only three times a week, and there was no way that I could go to visit Bill. The mail service was also deplorable. We were forced to use the telephone, although we presumed that the central telephone operator listened to our every word.

Bill's Cutknife duty took its toll from both of us. He had scarcely any work to do, which irked him and also gave him more time for brooding. He developed ulcers. As for me, nothing could replace my being with Bill. Besides, my chronic back problem had worsened from the strain of going to Maidstone almost every weekend for three months, and from my constantly being tired. My back went into painful spasm, and the medical doctors couldn't help me. I went to a chiropractor who had helped me before, but Bill didn't want me to continue because he'd heard that the chiropractor had a bad reputation. I was being helped, so I kept going, which made Bill's ulcers worse, which made me more tense.

Then one of Bill's usual twenty-page letters arrived, surprisingly joyful.

"I think I might see you soon," he wrote. "I'm finishing an investigation that Torrens started, and I think I'll probably have a prisoner. I can pick him up by snowplane, and bring him in to North Battleford by train. Here's hoping, darling."

"Here's hoping, darling," I echoed, thankful that Bill had located a so-called snowplane. Such vehicles were experimental, propeller-driven machines mounted on four skis. They could travel almost anywhere over snowbound, drift-covered rural Saskatchewan. (Later, snowplanes gave way to more serviceable vehicles with caterpillar drive.)

Unfortunately for us, Bill's prisoner didn't materialize. And the only other possible one chose to pay a fine rather than go to jail. We were quite provoked.

"Never mind," the central operator must have heard us say to each other scores of times. "It's not much more than a year to July 6, 1939."

Meanwhile we hoped that, after Bill's Cutknife period, the RCMP would let him stay in North Battleford for the next sixteen months. During that time he would concentrate on building up his savings to the $1,200 (value of any furniture and car included) that the Force insisted a man must have before he was allowed to marry. In those days that was about one year's salary for a first-class constable, but Bill would soon have that amount. We must stop feeling sad, and remember that marriage would solve all our problems. Oh, happy, happy July 6, 1939!

At the end of March, Bill returned to North Battleford and again we basked in the glow of contentment. In good spirits we resumed practicing for the coming festival. Bill won at North Battleford, and thus was entitled to compete further. So one Saturday morning we drove in his Ford coupé to Saskatoon. He was the only one in his class, but his good marks allowed him to enter the Northern finals later that day.

Bill was dismayed to learn that his competitors – a soprano, a contralto, a tenor and a bass – were all semi-professionals he had often heard on the Saskatoon radio station, CFQC, while he was stationed at Meadow Lake and Goodsoil.

"We might as well go home," he said despondently. "I can't compete against professionals. Let's go home and forget I ever entered the festival."

"Certainly not," I said firmly. "I'm sure you can hold your own against those other singers, no matter who they are. We'll stay!"

Reluctantly he agreed.

That night he sang and won again.

"The baritone won by a clear margin," the adjudicator

announced. His only criticism was that Bill should have put more emphasis on the last two notes. I wasn't at all surprised at Bill's victory, but of course I was as delighted as he was.

Soon after the festival the RCMP gave us another shock.

Bill had taken me to see the Walt Disney animated movie, *Snow White and the Seven Dwarfs*. The innovative style, the tuneful songs and the glowing colours fascinated me just as I knew they would fascinate the children I taught. Back at my apartment, I immediately stretched out on the bed to relax my aching back while we discussed the unusual film. Bill came over to sit on the edge of the bed and bent to kiss me.

"Darling," he murmured, "I have bad news. The Force has changed the marriage regulations. I now have to serve seven years before we can get married."

I burst into tears.

"I knew you'd take it like that," he said. "That's why I waited till after the show to tell you. I wanted you to enjoy the film."

Then the details. Bill had read the new regulations that morning in the weekly General Orders that mounties read avidly, if only to learn who among them had disgraced himself. He didn't know why the regulations had been changed. He did know, however, that some men would be allowed to marry under the former six-year rule, but only if the man was "irrevocably committed".

"We certainly should qualify," I said. "How could any two people be more irrevocably committed than we are?"

"It doesn't mean what you think it means," Bill said. "It means that the couple have bought their furniture. We haven't, so we can't get married in 1939."

"They can add more years whenever they like," I sniffled. "Maybe we'll never be allowed to get married."

"Oh, yes, we will," Bill said confidently. "But now we have to wait till July 6, 1940".

Years later I learned that "irrevocably committed" meant that the girl was pregnant, but that condition was too delicate for the RCMP to refer to it specifically in print. I also learned that Bill hadn't told me at the time in case I might try desperately to qualify, although he should have known better. In any case, if he had written to tell his superiors that he must get married because his fiancée was pregnant, he would almost certainly have been charged in orderly room with "cohabiting with a woman other than his wife". Then he surely would have been punished, probably by being dismissed.

It was a Catch-22 situation in which we couldn't win. Unless Bill left the RCMP, which was unthinkable, we could only wait for two more endless years, or even longer if the Force so decreed. Suddenly the future looked bleak.

Christmas, 1937, North Battleford. Bill and I had these photos taken to please each other.

NINE

When my mother returned to Vancouver for another holiday, in the summer of 1938, I moved into her apartment to spend the summer happily near Bill. One evening in mid-August, however, he brought disturbing news.

"I'm transferred to Maidstone!" he announced enthusiastically. "That detachment rates a corporal, so that means the OC believes I can handle a corporal's job!"

"That's great!" I meant it, but I was uneasy. "When are you leaving?"

"Right away! But I'll arrange for you to stay at the hotel for the rest of your summer holiday. After that you can come on weekends. How about it?"

"I don't like the idea," I complained. "It makes me feel like a camp follower. But I'll come."

The hotel in Maidstone, like many in small Saskatchewan towns then, was a box-like, two-storey frame building with a flat roof. Like the police detachment a few buildings away, it fronted the North Battleford-Lloydminster highway, and looked out on the town's little railway station and a row of grain elevators across the road.

My second floor room, for which Bill paid an inexpensive weekly rate, had little or no insulation from the elements. The blazing afternoon sun drove the outdoor temperatures into the high nineties Farenheit, and the heat in my room became unbearable. Patiently I adapted by stripping down to my panties and bra, and frequently splashing all my exposed skin with water from the big pottery pitcher on the rickety wooden washstand. Frequently, too, I sprinkled water on the linoleum-covered floor. As it evaporated in the dry Saskatchewan heat, it gradually cooled the room slightly. Then I often lay on my bed and read. Sometimes I sat at the shaky wooden table and practiced on my little portable typewriter, vaguely hoping that someday I might become a writer. But always I splashed and sprinkled.

As I came out of the hotel dining room one scorching hot day after a solitary lunch while Bill was away, I saw a pitiable young woman standing in the lobby. She was not wearing a hat, and her straight blonde hair looked wet with perspiration. Under her armpits large wet patches stained her short-sleeved gingham dress. Her legs were bare, her sensible oxfords scuffed and worn. At her feet lay a cheap-looking oversized suitcase, open to show what I supposed she was peddling. But she looked too slight, too exhausted, to carry it.

She told me she was selling lace tablecloths at ten dollars each. As I handled one of the lovely cloths of machine-made heavy lace, I wanted to buy it. I would add it to my "hope chest" of utilitarian lengths of unhemmed sheeting and pillowcasing that I was buying, thriftily, at wholesale through the provincial hospital.

"I'm sorry, but I only have four dollars," I said. "My fiancé has the rest of my money for safekeeping. He's a mountie and away working. But he expects to be back by three o'clock. If you come up to my room to rest till then, I can pay you the ten dollars."

We went up the stairs, but she wouldn't let me help carry her heavy suitcase.

"Lie on the bed and have a good rest," I suggested. But she wouldn't. Instead she sat awkwardly on the only chair, an uncomfortable wooden one. So after getting her a cold drink, I stretched out on the bed.

"I know how you must feel," I said, hoping to make her feel more at ease. "The summer I was fourteen I worked in Woolworth's on Saturdays. Ten hours at twenty cents an hour. I walked about ten blocks in the dreadful heat to go home for lunch and again for supper. Often it was so hot that while I ate my meals, I soaked my swollen feet in a bowl of cool water that my mother set out for me."

"I never would have thought you had gone through hard times," the girl said.

"I was lucky," I said. "I hope you will be too."

When Bill wasn't back at half past three, the girl couldn't wait any longer.

"You can have the tablecloth for four dollars," she said.

I protested, but she insisted.

"I'd like you to have it," she said. "You've been so kind. I've never met anybody like you."

So she had my four dollars, and I had her lovely tablecloth.

When Bill came back I told him all about the hot, careworn girl, and that she couldn't wait for the money.

"Huh!" Bill scoffed. "She couldn't wait because she knew I was a policeman. She was probably peddling without a license, and she knew I'd run her out of town."

We had our first bitter argument. At last I stopped trying to persuade Bill that the girl should be pitied, not censured. I decided that his suspicious, callous attitude came with his job.

When September called me back to teaching again, I made tiring weekend trips to visit Bill. One weekend in early fall I found that the detachment had been moved, on government orders, to a better house, where a lean-to would serve as a more convenient office.

Then young Constable Lorne Cawsey, a dogmaster, arrived with his handsome ninety-pound German Shepherd, Dale of Cawsalta. Dale was a remarkable dog, the first ever used by a member of the RCMP as a police service dog. He was not the first to be owned by the Force: that honour went to Dale's son, Black Lux. But Dale, who originally belonged to Lorne's father, Sergeant J.N. Cawsey in Alberta, had done such amazing work for the sergeant that the RCMP persuaded him to let them buy Dale.

Lorne had grown up with Dale, and after taking the regular RCMP training, he became a dogmaster, with Dale as his working dog. The two of them would help Bill, and any other mountie on request, to track suspected criminals, find lost persons, and seek and find would-be safe-crackers, hiding before breaking into the safes of grain elevators and stores. Incidentally, unemployed men no longer rode illegally in boxcars: presumably they were in work camps.

While Bill and Lorne supervised the building of Dale's living quarters, a huge wooden kennel and a twenty-foot, fenced-in runway, the dog lived in the house with the men. During the daytime at weekends, after the men had finished their work, I often became a temporary fourth member of their establishment. We all used to assemble in the only room of the house used by the men, the living room, which they also used as their bedroom. There we listened to the radio owned jointly by Bill and Lorne, or to Lorne's stories about his much-loved dog. In the absence of comfortable chairs, Lorne stretched out on his police-issue bed, while Bill and I stretched out on Bill's. Dale stretched out, full length, on the floor between the beds.

When we listened to the radio, Dale paid no attention to any talk program. But when he heard music, including the songs of Bill's favourite, Nelson Eddy, he put his head on his outstretched front paws and seemed to listen intently. Whenever Lorne's favourite, Bing Crosby, came on, Dale rolled over on his back. Curling his front paws close to his chest, he whined a sing-along-with-Bing as long as the crooner was on the air.

Lorne's stories about Dale were fascinating. The dog had learned more skills than any other police service dog of that time. He could track, guard, warn his master of danger, ward off an attacker, jump through open windows, climb ladders, scale an eight-foot-high wooden obstacle that seemed to have no footholds and perform many other tasks.

Dale had also learned that if he didn't obey commands, he would be punished. One day when Lorne was exercising the dog off leash in a field, the German Shepherd ignored his master's command to return, and dashed after a rabbit. A few moments later he stopped in mid-chase. Then he lowered himself to his belly and crawled in penitence, punishing himself in the way Lorne would have punished him.

One of Dale's earliest notable cases began in November 1933, when Sergeant Cawsey took the dog with him and a constable to investigate a stolen car abandoned in a field near Gleichen, Alberta. Dale followed square-toed footprints through slushy snow, from the car to a nearby cabin. There the mounties found a sleeping man with square-toed shoes near him. They took the shoes, and made plaster casts of the footprints, thinking they had enough evidence to convict the man of stealing the car. The judge hearing the case, however, found the man not guilty. He said that no Canadian court of law recognized evidence provided by a dog.

Nevertheless, Cawsey continued to use Dale. He tracked an arsonist although the scent was old and mixed with the strong fumes of gasoline. He found money lost by a child whose mother had given it to her to pay a relief bill. Once the big dog chased, without command, a dollar bill he saw blowing in the wind. Then, still without command, he sniffed out the man who had the same scent, and offered him the bill. In 1934 he saved the lives of his master and a constable when their car broke down in a blinding mid-winter blizzard.

In 1935 he found a lost child in a field of tall wheat where a hundred men had searched in vain for many hours. For this feat, which undoubtedly saved the little girl's life, a Chicago magazine made Dale a member of the Legion of Honour of the Dog World of the United States.

Later in 1935, the RCMP bought the remarkable Dale of Cawsalta, and he became Police Service Dog Regimental Number K470 ("K" Division, Alberta). He had his own living allowance and his own personal file, just like the two-footed mounties.

The more I heard about Dale of Cawsalta, the more I realized what a remarkable creature he was. I decided to put into practice some of the things I had learned through the correspondence course in newspaper writing I had taken during one summer holiday. I had written a lot of pieces for practice, but had never tried to sell anything. Now I decided to try to sell an article on Dale. I queried *Maclean's* magazine. The editor answered immediately. The magazine had just commissioned an article on the training school for police service dogs that RCMP Commissioner (later Sir) James MacBrien had recently established. The editor could use a supplementary 1,200-word article about Dale.

Lorne was as thrilled as I was. But Bill objected.

"I don't want you getting involved in Mounted Police affairs!" he said curtly.

"I'm going to do the article anyway," I said firmly.

"Then you'll have to get the OC's permission," he said.

Resentfully I did so. Soon I had the article in the mail to *Maclean's*. With it, because my newspaper course stressed the value of pictures, and because I was a keen snapshot enthusiast, I also sent my handsome headshot of Dale. Before long *Maclean's* accepted both, and sent me a cheque for thirty dollars, presumably about two cents a word for the article and five dollars for the picture.

Lorne and I, elated, eagerly awaited publication. But Bill was noncommittal.

Meanwhile, as a teacher during the depression, I had found it hard to acquire funds for such extras as children's songs, plays, recitations and so on. I used to buy whatever I could through the catalogue of the School Publications Company in Hamilton, Ontario, and I wrote other things myself. After *Maclean's* accepted my Dale article, Bill began urging me to try to sell some of my work to School Publications. I was touched by his faith in my ability, but later I wondered if he might have been trying to steer me away from RCMP topics.

I sent three little songs, words and melody only, to School Publications, explaining that they were based on pieces in the new readers for Grades 1, 2 and 3. Would they publish such songs? Editor Belva Howatt replied that she would like a set of thirty, with piano accompaniments if possible. That was no problem. I began writing the songs.

Thinking back to the winter of 1938-39, I wonder how I found the energy to do anything but teach. My back problem was so much worse that I had to do my lesson preparation lying down. But I still visited Bill at Maidstone. In fact, I felt contented only when I was with Bill.

Bill, Lorne and I patronized the weekend movies in the community hall, sitting on wooden benches and waiting patiently when the projection operator stopped his machine every two reels to change the film spools. When Bill and Lorne took part in a community concert, so did I. Bill rented a piano, which was shockingly out of tune. At my suggestion, he borrowed a tuning wrench from a man at nearby McLaren who had shown me how to use it when I taught there. Then I tuned that pitiably neglected instrument, and at weekends Bill sang to his heart's content, until my back gave out.

That winter of 1938-39 was so cold at night that a thick coating of ice formed in the big pitcher on my hotel washstand. Sometimes I travelled to Maidstone wearing the same clothing I'd worn a few years earlier when walking or riding horseback to my one-room school at Brightsand Lake. Layer on layer I donned: long woollen underwear, breeches, sweaters, two pairs of woollen socks, moccasins and a close-fitting cap with earflaps. Finally I put on a red Hudson's Bay blanket-cloth jacket that I had warmly lined and windproofed with chamois, bought by the yard through Eaton's catalogue. When Bill and I exercised by walking along the snow-plowed highway, our only possible route, we probably looked from a distance like a big mountie and a little one.

Any hardships seemed worthwhile, however. We had each other, plus music, books and good radio programs. We even developed a common interest in art through the Montreal *Star* newspaper. Bill returned each weekly coupon, with ten cents, to acquire prints of world-famous paintings and art appreciation booklets. The prints, averaging about nine by twelve inches, were faithfully reproduced, and the booklets were full of fascinating information.

During the winter, in spite of difficulties, I finished my book of songs, although I was so far behind schedule that I let my mother and Bill write some of the words, Mom for six songs and Bill for three. Miss Howatt accepted the book at once, and asked if I would like royalties or $100 as payment in full. $100 was more than I earned in a month, and it was offered for what I would have enjoyed doing without any payment. I took the cash.

I was thrilled, of course, but I didn't recognize it as a special achievement. Neither did I see it as anything special that my first published article had appeared in the highly-regarded *Maclean's* magazine. Decades later, however, as I checked my memorabilia, I saw that my article lay with distinguished company. That issue of March 1, 1939, contained a story by Bruce Hutchison, a long article on Raymond Massey by Merrill Denison, the monthly London Letter by Beverly Baxter, and other pieces by well-known writers. My photo of Dale had the place of honour at the top of the full-length dog-school article. And although my 1,200 words were placed at the end of the long article, mine had their own title, "Dale of Cawsalta", and my name was in bold black lettering. Moreover, my piece was printed exactly as I had sent it, with not even a comma changed, although in those days I presumed, naively, that was what always happened.

On publication I felt so buoyed up that I immediately followed another piece of advice from my newspaper course. I initiated a writing job for myself.

The Saskatoon *Star-Phoenix* used country correspondents as well as staff writers. But the Provincial Hospital, which was a vibrant community, had no correspondent. *Star-Phoenix* editor A.H. Walls agreed that I should be the country correspondent for the hospital community, and said I would be paid ten cents per column inch. That seems ridiculously low today, but at the time one inch of copy would buy two *Maclean's* magazines, which were only five cents each.

There was plenty to write about, and Mr. Walls printed, with absolutely no changes, whatever I sent. The hospital farm raised a special breed of pigs. The poultry section raised and released thousands of game birds, including beautifully coloured pheasants. The farm bought an additional 300 acres, cleared the land with a diesel tractor (rare in those days), and set about installing an irrigation system. School classes listened to a talk on bee keeping, and to another talk by a man who had made a trip on the then-famous Queen Elizabeth ocean liner. Nurses were graduated, and church ladies gave teas and bake sales. Retiring employees were honoured at farewell parties, senior doctors gave important speeches, and the Choral Group entered the music festival. Writing possibilities were endless.

I was a Saskatoon *Star-Phoenix* country correspondent during April, May and June, and in May, my best month, the newspaper published thirty-one column inches of my writing. What pleased me most, however, was that I had created the position for myself.

Winter, 1937-38, North Battleford. My mother and I are outside the building where she had an apartment.

Early winter, 1938, Maidstone. Bill is in red serge uniform. The star on his sleeve indicates that he has completed five years' service. I am wearing my black electric seal (dyed-rabbit) fur coat with matching muff, a deep rose felt hat with silver feather, and lace-up velvet overshoes.

1938, Maidstone.
Dogmaster Constable
Lorne Cawsey with his
much-loved dog, Dale of
Cawsalta, beside Dale's
kennel and its
wire-covered runway.

1938, Maidstone. My photo of Dale
of Cawsalta, used with my article
about Dale in Maclean's Magazine,
March 1939.

TEN

Meanwhile, the RCMP had disrupted our lives again. "I've been transferred to Hafford," Bill announced as he met me at the Maidstone railway station one Friday night.

Again it was a good move. He would be in charge of the two-man detachment in that small town about forty miles east of North Battleford. Unfortunately, Bill could come to North Battleford only if his work demanded it, and I could visit him only if I travelled, uncomfortably, by bus.

I went once, but I might as well have stayed at home. Bill's hours of duty exceeded even those at Goodsoil. In fact, the Hafford detachment area covered a settled district of Ukrainians, Poles, Russians, Germans, French and English on quarter-section farms. Incidentally, on one of the English farms lived a young boy who later became Commissioner Robert Symonds of the RCMP.

Police duties at Hafford kept both Bill and his junior constable fully occupied. Day and night they investigated theft, fraud, mischief, family quarrels, disputes about fences, and the making and selling of home brew. They also made frequent highway patrols, took mental patients to hospital and investigated suicides.

Bill's most unusual duty at Hafford occurred while King George VI and Queen Elizabeth (later the Queen Mother), made their 1939 cross-country tour of Canada. Bill checked a switch on a railway that ran through open fields. The switch had already been secured, and

Bill found it had not been tampered with. Then he stood at attention as the Royal train, blinds drawn, sped past. Bill, standing about two hundred yards from the railroad, heard a squeak and found he was not alone. A gopher, also at attention a few yards away, sat on its haunches and watched the train go by.

During that same Royal tour, Constable Lorne Cawsey and Dale travelled to Unity, a small Saskatchewan town where the Royal train would make a brief stop. Lorne and Dale pushed their way through the waiting crowds, and Dale thoroughly searched all boxcars near the depot where the train would arrive.

About two months later, the eight-year-old German Shepherd showed signs of rheumatism and a strained heart. A board of RCMP officers discussed Dale just as they would have discussed a human policeman. They found the remarkable dog unfit for further service, and ordered him returned to his original owner, Sergeant Cawsey. In special recognition of his outstanding work, they established a precedent by granting him a small pension to cover the cost of his food. Although Dale's work was never recognized by a Canadian court of law, it laid the foundation for the acceptance of other dogs' work. In fact, the first case in which evidence produced by a dog was accepted in a Canadian court occurred in February 1940. The dog involved was Black Lux, son of Dale.

Meanwhile, Bill did his best to get from Hafford to North Battleford occasionally, but he seldom succeeded. Nevertheless, one rain-drenched day he came to see me in spite of his patrol sergeant's refusal to authorize the trip. The roads that day were so bad that the sergeant had travelled to Hafford by bus rather than by police car. Bill, alert as usual, offered to drive him back to North Battleford.

"Anyway, sarge," Bill explained truthfully, "the Hafford police car has been troublesome, and the nearest place to do the necessary repairs is the dealer's shop at North Battleford. So let me drive you back."

"No thanks!" the sergeant snapped. "You're just looking for an excuse to see your girlfriend!"

As soon as the patrol sergeant boarded the bus for North Battleford, Bill telephoned Staff Sergeant S. at the sub/division office there. He knew that the two NCOs hated each other, so he explained to S. that the Hafford car needed repairs, but the patrol sergeant wouldn't authorize the necessary trip to North Battleford. The staff sergeant, senior to the patrol sergeant, authorized the trip without question. Within fifteen minutes of the patrol sergeant's departure, Bill was on the road.

Driving on the slippery, mud-coated gravel proved difficult, but

Bill had no great trouble. The bus driver didn't do as well. About halfway to North Battleford Bill saw the bus pulled in at a service station. The hood was up, with clouds of steam issuing from the radiator. Apparently the driver was waiting for an overworked engine to cool. Bill pretended not to see, and drove on. When the patrol sergeant arrived at the North Battleford detachment, Bill was already there.

"How the hell did you get here?" the patrol sergeant shouted.

"I needed car repairs, so I phoned Staff Sergeant S. for permission," Bill replied calmly. Then, because the car wouldn't be ready till the next morning, he didn't need permission to stay in the city overnight or to visit me.

Bill would never have risked antagonizing his patrol sergeant if he hadn't been so unhappy with Mounted Police restrictions. Many years later, however, we learned that Bill's stay at Hafford had been for good reason. His former OC, by then retired as Superintendent Spriggs, explained it to us on the same occasion at which we discussed the glory-seeking Detective Sergeant B. Spriggs said he had marked his two outstanding constables, Bill and Lloyd Bingham, as officer material. Bill's frequent moves were intended to give him varied experience. Moreover, Spriggs had sent him to Hafford because that detachment had married quarters that we could occupy as soon as Bill was allowed to marry.

In those days, however, it was not the habit of senior officers to inform their juniors that they were promising material. Neither did the RCMP have a Personnel Department to consider the problems of constables and NCOs, and to advise them. So Bill was unhappy and even, at times, despondent.

As for me, I became depressed. I not only missed Bill dreadfully, but the condition of my back had deteriorated. At recess times at school I had to lie on a cloakroom bench to relax enough to carry on. And because sitting was my most tiresome position, I had to mark exercise books standing up, using the top of the piano instead of my desk. I knew I couldn't continue teaching. At the end of May I gave the required month's notice, and resigned.

Of course I also had to resign from my job as country correspondent for the Saskatoon *Star-Phoenix*. When I did so I sent my editor a copy of my *Highroads to Singing*. It was an attractive eight by twelve-inch book, with three little birds singing on the bright blue cover, and with black and white illustrations. Mr. Walls published a seven-inch column praising the book, then wrote to tell me he was surprised and pleased at the "excellence" of both words and music. He had shown it to several city teachers, including some who taught music in the schools, and they also admired it. One of them offered to promote it among other teachers, and to bring it to the attention of the superintendent of the Saskatoon schools.

My pupils, too, were pleased with *Highroads to Singing*. After Grade 2 had learned "Long Ago", a song about Canadian Indians, we all did a war dance around the classroom. After the Grade 3 children read "Pig and Pepper", a segment of *Alice in Wonderland*, in which somebody puts too much pepper in the soup, everyone learned the song of the same name. My mother had written the words, and had put in numerous "Ah-choo!" sneezes, which we all performed with intense enthusiasm. Incidentally, as soon as I received my $100.00 payment, I insisted on giving my mother a fair share for her six poems, but I didn't offer Bill anything.

My last item in the *Star-Phoenix* was a short account of my own farewell party, a tea at which the ladies of the hospital community presented me with a silver-plated cake plate and a casserole in a heavily plated silver holder. They also thanked me for my four years of caring service to the children, who would miss me sadly. I didn't mention those thanks in my column, or that I was so deeply touched that I had a lump in my throat.

Neither did I mention that I would sadly miss the children, but as I thought of them my heart grew heavy. Would my replacement take the trouble to write to the soap company that gave, on request, miniature bars of soap, one for each child? Would she write to the toothpaste company that, also on request, gave small tubes of toothpaste? And if she did so, would she make calendar-like forms for the children to note that they had cleaned their teeth after meals, washed their hands after visiting the toilet, had the required hours of sleep, and so on? Would she praise them even if they didn't achieve perfection, and encourage self-esteem by sticking gold stars on the charts of children who had done their best?

Would my replacement empathize with children like six-year-old Kenny, a normally happy child who one day grew angry for no apparent reason and hurled an inkwell at his best friend? The other children, also upset, explained that Kenny, formerly an only child, was unhappy because his mother had just had a baby. I went home with the unhappy child after school, and together with his mother we worked things out. Not only Kenny, but the other children, too, returned to their happy normal selves.

Would I ever again know a child like seven-year-old Isobel, who took her party candy home instead of eating it at our parties because her doctor father said that she should eat candy only after meals? Would my replacement even know that Isobel was an only, privileged child who willingly shared her Christmas and birthday gifts with underprivileged children?

How could I fail to miss the pretty little eight-year-old identical twin girls who could easily have confused me but never did? And what about the two boys, now ten years old, whose first day at the hospital school had coincided with mine? I had guided the scholastic facets of their development from Grade 1 through Grade 4, until I felt like their part-time parent. Of course I didn't mention such things in my column, or that as I thanked the ladies for their kindness, I'd had to dab my tear-filled eyes with my handkerchief.

Meanwhile, after I had resigned, Bill and I confronted the problem of our desperate unhappiness at being kept apart by RCMP Rules and Regulations. We planned that if he could get leave during the summer, we would go to Toronto and get expert advice about his voice and his chance of a professional singing career. If the advice was favourable, as I believed it would be, he would ask for a transfer to Toronto. If the transfer came through, he would study singing in his off-duty hours. I, too, would go to Toronto, where I could probably get specialized treatment for my back. When the time seemed opportune, Bill would buy his way out of the Force, and we'd get married.

If the Force wouldn't give Bill the transfer, he would leave it sooner, go to Toronto, get a job with the Toronto city police, and study singing in his free time.

Either way, purchasing his discharge might be expensive. In those days men could engage or re-engage for one, three or five years. Bill had optimistically chosen five years each time, so in 1939 he still had four years to serve. Forty-eight months of repayment at three dollars a month, or $144, wouldn't be a burden. But the commissioner could order him to repay any expense the Force had incurred in connection with him. Would the commissioner charge for Bill's recruit training? For his uniforms over the years? Anyway, whatever the price, we'd gladly pay it if we could transfer ourselves to a freer, happier life together.

Bill was granted three weeks leave in July, and he told his fellow mounties that we were going to Toronto for a holiday. Some of them presumed we were going there to be married secretly. They probably knew that one constable, recently granted leave and permission to marry, had arrived back at his detachment with his wife and their three-year-old daughter. Another constable and his "fiancée", so we learned later, had an elaborate church wedding in 1940, but had been secretly married after the marriage regulations had been changed in 1938.

Bill and I, however, were not going to Toronto to be married. We were taking the first step toward leaving the Royal Canadian Mounted Police.

The teacher.

Teacher and Pupils

Gilbert and friend.

A grade 1 charmer.

At Hallowe'en.

Kenny and friend.

A joint project.

A grade 2 student.

ELEVEN

The city of Toronto entranced both Bill and me, an unsophisticated couple from the prairies. We checked in at the reputable Walker House, circumspectly in different rooms, but convenient for visiting. Then we began to cram new experiences into our three weeks' holiday. We savoured art galleries, museums, the Promenade concerts, big department stores, Ringling Brothers' Circus, and a palatial movie theatre with a throbbing pipe organ that rose from underground depths. We stared at everything, from the huge pulsating neon signs advertising White Rose gasoline and Neilson's chocolates, to the graceful trees, especially the stately elms arching over the residential streets.

First, though, we sought an opinion about Bill's voice. I had presumed that he would go to the prestigious Toronto Conservatory of Music, to which my piano and theory teachers belonged, and from which I had earned my music certificate. But he went to see Mr. M., who had a studio on Yonge Street.

"A splendid voice! Excellent possibilities for a singing career!" the suave, distinguished-looking man said. "You need to produce your voice more correctly, Mr. Kelly, but I could help you with that."

He demonstrated, breathing from the diaphragm to give solid support for the voice. Bill did the same, and was persuaded. I felt a vague distrust of Mr. M.'s ingratiating charm, but his method seemed reasonable. Eagerly Bill agreed to take several lessons a week during our holiday, and if possible to return for more.

Next we sought advice from a senior orthopedic surgeon at the renowned Sick Children's Hospital.

"There's nothing wrong with your back," he said, although he could see that my spine curved abnormally, creating bulging muscles on my left side and a shrunken hollow on my right. "Lots of people are one-sided. Just go home and be happy."

Instead I checked chiropractors' advertisements in the Toronto telephone book, and chose the most informative.

The next day Dr. Clubine performed a near-miracle. He draped me over a large wooden wheel for ten minutes, and when I got off it I could stand normally for the first time in many months. The effect lasted only about a minute, but it indicated that I didn't have to become a helpless cripple.

"I must ask for that transfer," Bill declared.

On returning home, I stayed with my mother while Bill went back to Hafford. He discussed the transfer with the sympathetic Inspector Spriggs, who advised him how to proceed. To our delight the transfer was granted, to take place in September. Life held happiness after all.

Then, on September 1, Germany attacked Poland. On September 3, Britain declared war on Germany. A week later, Canada entered the war to support Britain.

My mother and I were enjoying a leisurely Sunday breakfast when we heard the news over the radio. I gasped with apprehension. Would Bill join the fray of senseless destruction, pain and death? No! The news announcer was saying that the RCMP would be "frozen". Would Bill be "frozen" at Hafford? Within a few days, however, we learned that his transfer would take place as planned.

Years later, as I researched the history of the Force, I learned why Bill's transfer had been granted. Ever since Commissioner S.T. Wood took office in March 1938, he had directed the Force in anticipation of the war. The Force positioned its men accordingly so that at a moment's notice they could arrest known Nazi sympathizers and guard vital points. Commissioner Wood also anticipated sabotage and war crimes, especially in large cities, so he ordered the number of Mounted Police in such cities to be increased. Men like Bill, with criminal investigative experience in the west, were needed in Ontario, although by the beginning of October he was still at Hafford.

Meanwhile, in mid-September I had moved to Toronto to begin chiropractic treatments. By that time my back was in painful spasm. I could still walk, but with difficulty.

During my first week in Toronto I stayed at a downtown hotel while I shuffled the few blocks to Dr. Clubine's office on Richmond Street each day. At that time I couldn't travel by streetcar because the steps were too high. But I noticed that an Eaton's bus travelled between the Eaton's store at Queen and Yonge streets and the one at College and Yonge. I found that I could step into the bus, and that it was a free service for customers. So I checked the rooming houses near College and Yonge, and rented a room with Miss McFayden on McGill street. Then I travelled to and from my treatments courtesy of Eaton's. But I didn't feel guilty, as I had been a faithful mail-order customer for years.

The treatments helped me only slightly at first, but I remembered the wheel, and I remained hopeful.

Painfully I shuffled from place to place, enjoying everything within my range: movies, art galleries, concerts at Massey Hall and special exhibitions anywhere. At every opportunity I sat and rested, on Dr. Clubine's advice leaning against a small cushion I carried everywhere, and slipping a small notebook under my left buttock to prop up my heavy side.

Nevertheless, as my letters indicated, I began to worry that the Force might keep Bill in Saskatchewan.

"You've turned Nora into a clinging vine," my self-reliant mother told Bill when police duties took him to North Battleford. "The sooner you go to Toronto the better."

He came in mid-October. By chance he was billeted at the RCMP Charles Street barracks above the post office on Yonge Street, two blocks from where I roomed.

"Life is good," we said to each other again and again, glad that Miss McFayden didn't insist on my leaving my door ajar when I had a visitor, as some landladies did then.

On Monday, October 16, Bill reported for duty at "O" Division (Western Ontario) headquarters at Bay and Front Streets. In view of his requesting the transfer, he was apprehensive that he might be given routine work where he'd have to wear a uniform. So he was very pleased when he was ordered to report to the Criminal Investigation Branch (CIB). And because the Force in Ontario did federal policing only, unlike in Saskatchewan where it did both federal and provincial work, Bill anticipated interesting cases. The Force's work included the enforcement of the regulations emanating from the federally imposed War Measures Act, and assisting federal government departments which had acquired new responsibilities connected with the war. There would be plenty of interesting work for Bill to do.

Even so, he planned that after work he could fit in several

singing lessons weekly, and that we could eat our evening meals together at a nearby restaurant.

After Bill's pleasure at being taken into the CIB, he was rather taken aback when Detective Sergeant Maxwell Veitch of the CIB handed him several streetcar tickets, and told him he'd be travelling by streetcar while he got to know the city. Luckily, that method of travel gave Bill his first small success in Toronto.

Together with the streetcar tickets, Sergeant Veitch had given Bill several "mug-shot" photos of wanted criminals.

"We haven't had any luck with these," Veitch said, "but you never know."

As Bill travelled north on Yonge Street while on an investigation a few days later, he sat across the aisle from a man he thought he recognized. He was about to ask the man if they had met, when he thought of the mug shots in the briefcase between his feet. Surreptitiously he studied the photos. One of them showed what looked like a younger version of the man across the aisle. On the back was the information that he was a safe-blower for whom the Manitoba RCMP had issued a warrant three years earlier.

When the man got off the streetcar at one of the two exits, Bill got off at the other, and followed him. After a second streetcar ride and a short walk, the man entered a house. Bill didn't dare arrest him in case he had the wrong man, so he rushed to a pay phone and called Sergeant Veitch. When the sergeant arrived, the two of them entered the house, found he was the wanted man, and arrested him.

Bill was paraded and commended by the Officer in Command of the whole division. At suppertime that evening he reported the incident to me. I was elated. My mountie had apparently begun doing notable work in Ontario, just as he had done in the west! This was certainly a good start in his new division.

Soon after the streetcar incident, Bill helped Sergeant Veitch investigate a passport fraud. The case concerned Mr. M., a man from Europe who had tried to enter Canada illegally, assisted by a young Canadian woman who had fallen in love with him. In court the woman pleaded guilty, and the sympathetic magistrate gave her a suspended sentence, so she was free to leave. Mr. M. was found guilty and ordered deported. He remained under arrest, and Bill and another constable led him from the courtroom. In the hall Mr. M. caught a glimpse of the young woman.

"Hello, darling," he called. He seemed to want to pause for a chat, but the two mounties escorted him away.

That same day the Toronto *Star* carried a two-column report of the case, with pictures. One of them showed Bill, in civvies for CIB work, looking young and handsome in his dark fedora as he grasped the protesting Mr. M. by the arm.

Bill and I were delighted. How much more exciting was Toronto than Saskatchewan with its petty crimes and no publicity! I immediately started a "BILL" scrapbook.

Soon he was working alone, investigating the possible counterfeiting of Canadian banknotes. Mr. L., a Rumanian, admitted that he had written to a New York company asking about the manufacture of banknotes.

"But I did it for my friend Joe," he insisted.

Later Bill searched his apartment and found lithographing stones, 250-watt bulbs, and some coloured bulbs necessary to take a print from the unwrinkled genuine ten dollar bill he had in a frame.

"But I bought them with Joe's money," Mr. L. declared. "So they don't belong to me. They belong to Joe."

The magistrate in No. 2 Police Court didn't believe him, and found him guilty of possessing instruments for the manufacture of Canadian banknotes. The Toronto *Telegram* carried a detailed account of the case, and I promptly pasted a second clipping in my scrapbook.

Christmas that year was the best we'd had together. We heaped delicatessen goodies on the little table in my room, with the overflow spread on the dresser. Then, slowly and carefully, I seated myself on the only chair, supported by my cushion and notebook, while Bill perched cheerfully on the edge of the bed. After toasting each other with milk in paper cups, we feasted from paper plates.

Later, snuggled together on Miss McFayden's sagging three-quarter-size bed, we counted our blessings. My back was improving. Bill's singing was going well. Then he told me his special news. A fellow mountie, a married man, would soon be transferred. Bill could sublet his apartment, only a block away. Bill could buy his furniture, and we would buy a secondhand piano to complete our household establishment. I could move into "our" apartment on the first of February. Happy Christmas!

A week later we celebrated New Year's Day by going to a movie near enough for me to walk. On that notable evening we had even more cause to rejoice. Up to that time, after I had sat through a movie I had to lie down on the restroom couch, and if there was no couch I had to lie on the floor. When I stood up to leave the theatre on New Year's Day 1940, however, I knew I didn't need to lie down. As we made our way back to Miss McFayden's, I could still only shuffle along, holding Bill's arm for support, but I knew I had reached the turning point. Life was indeed good!

Soon I could step into a streetcar. I travelled the city till I found a splendid used Nordheimer piano, a large walnut upright with an excellent tone. Bill gave his cheque for $250 (my savings were almost gone). Our piano would be delivered on request.

On the morning of February 1, I moved into the apartment on Isabella Street. There our furniture, which Bill had bought from his mountie friend for five dollars, awaited me: two tables, two chairs, and a davenport that pulled out to make a double bed. Two beautiful down pillows lay on the davenport, and I thought how generous Bill's friend was. That afternoon, however, Mrs. Mountie came for the pillows she had left by mistake. The next day the janitor came to claim one of the tables. Many years later, when Bill was painting the two chairs and the other table because they were too good to discard, he found the undersides marked: Property of Such and Such Parish Church Hall.

We also had bad luck with the piano when we asked the owner of the apartment house when it would be convenient to have it delivered.

"Sorry!" he said emphatically. "We don't allow pianos! The last one nearly drove us crazy!"

On March 1, I moved from Isabella Street and settled in at Coral Gables on Wellesley Street, again not far from Bill's barracks. This time we were in luck. The building was almost soundproof, and the caretaker had told us we could make music without reservation.

Happiness reigned during the next four months. Bill's work increased, but he tackled it with enthusiasm. He still found time for singing lessons several times a week, though sometimes late at night, and his resonant baritone voice was developing upward to include some fine tenor sounds. At last he, too, believed he could aim at a singing career.

"After the war," we assured each other.

Meanwhile my improved mobility allowed me to discover the splendid public library and the extensive reference library on George Street, within easy reach by streetcar. I also discovered the free daytime lectures at the Toronto Conservatory of Music, and the free organ concerts there, given by Dr. Healy Willan, whose choral and other compositions I had long admired.

Might I be advanced enough in music for Dr. Willan to teach me composition? One day in mid-March I found the courage to go to the Conservatory to ask him. He encouraged me to tell him not only about my musical background, but also my personal life. He agreed to teach me, beginning with a course of thirteen lessons, then suggested I should write songs for Bill.

Those composition lessons with Dr. Willan gave me some of the happiest hours of my life. He treated me as an intelligent person as he guided me: choose a poem, study the rhythm of the words, and use that as a basis for the rhythm of the music. Finally, write the music in such keys and in such modes as to enhance the meaning of the words and the mood of my poem. It was what I'd done instinctively when writing my book of songs, but of course they were so simple.

I thrilled to Dr. Willan's logical approach, just as I had thrilled to the logic of mathematics and science in high school. After a few exercises, I worked on the poem *Wanderthirst*, by Gerald Gould. I tried to express the poem's uneasy longing and wanderlust, and I ended defiantly on Bill's highest pure note. Dr. Willan was pleased and so, therefore, was I.

"It's a marvellous song," Bill said. But he found it rather difficult, and was too busy to learn it just then. So I put it aside.

When my series of lessons ended about the middle of June, I said goodbye to Dr. Willan with pangs of regret, explaining that I had to prepare for my coming wedding. The truth was, Bill had been paying my expenses since my savings ran out, and he couldn't afford to keep paying for my lessons as well as his own, which of course were more important. Instead of fretting, I immediately began writing another song for him. This one was light and frivolous, *A Tragic Story*, by William Makepeace Thackeray, about an ancient Chinese sage who tried to make his pigtail hang in front instead of behind him.

It was surprising that Bill could find any time for singing. Although the RCMP had re-engaged ex-members and pensioners, and had hired Special Constable Guards, its regular members had much extra work. This included enforcing the new Defense of Canada Regulations, keeping track of enemy aliens, registering or re-registering firearms, and investigating possible subversion and sabotage. Making matters worse, the Force now had slightly fewer than the 2,600 regular members it had for the whole of Canada before the war. Some men whose time had expired had joined the army. The Marine and Aviation Sections of the RCMP had been transferred to the armed forces. The No. 1 Provost Company, RCMP, had been formed for services overseas.

No wonder the Mounted Police at home had to do double duty or more. And no wonder that when Bill came to Coral Gables for supper, he came less and less frequently, later and later.

He considered all his work important, but one investigation in the spring of 1940 was outstanding. A patriotic woman who worked for an engineering company in Welland, Ontario, had reported something suspicious. Americans working in the Canadian Welland company visited Canadian war plants to get orders for furnaces. In getting an order they had to find out what the war plant manufactured, what kind of furnace it used, the size of the plant, and for what output the furnace was needed.

The Welland company, however, was a subsidiary of an American company at Salem, Ohio, and all details of the orders went from Welland to Salem. And because the head of the Salem company was also the owner of an engineering company in Berlin, the informant suspected that information about Canadian war plants was being sent to our German enemies.

Bill's investigation proved that the informant's suspicions were justified. His report led the federal government to prohibit all Canadian manufacturing plants from dealing with the Welland company, so it was forced out of business. I was happy that Bill had so effectively helped the war effort. But there was no publicity, so I didn't have another clipping for my scrapbook.

Neither did I have one after he successfully investigated, for the Department of Immigration, an American illegally in Canada to sell and manipulate stocks in fraudulent mining companies. Because of Bill's work, the American was deported, and I had to be content with knowing that there was one less criminal in Canada. The identity of the informant had not been disclosed, but I presumed that the informant, like the Welland woman, was a loyal Canadian.

"More likely the informant was another bucket shop operator," Bill said cynically, "and he wanted to run his competition out of business."

When Italy entered the war in June 1940, the Force was well prepared, just as it had been in September 1939. Bill, like many mounties across Canada, helped arrest Italians deemed by government advisors to be possibly dangerous, and to register others as enemy aliens. Again there was no sabotage in Canada. And again, now that both German and Italian enemy aliens must be supervised, the work of the Force increased.

TWELVE

M eanwhile, Bill and I kept our emotional sights on July 6 and marriage. In April, three months in advance of that date and in accord with Rules and Regulations, he applied for permission to marry.

However, "Permission will only be granted to those members who by their conduct, efficiency, zeal and seniority have demonstrated their value to the Force," warned R. and R. as amended in 1938 to prevent marriages, including ours.

Bill's OC, Superintendent W. Schutz, forwarded his application to Commissioner S.T. Wood, with comments on Bill's satisfactory performance of his duties, and on his assets of $1,200. On a more personal note, but also in accord with R. and R., the OC's letter assured the commissioner that Regimental Number 12001, Constable Kelly, W.H., did indeed have "prior realization of the responsibility of marriage". Unfortunately, I was never able to find out what form of marital responsibility, if any, Bill and his OC discussed. Sexual? Financial? Helping with the children and the dishes?

Bill also had to give the names and addresses of his intended wife and her next of kin, so that the Force could find out if I were "a suitable person to live in government quarters". I resented the evaluation of my worthiness. The sooner Bill left the snobbish, autocratic RCMP the better!

I learned later that the Force was only ensuring that the intended wife would not "bring the Force into disrepute". She might be the close relative of a persistent criminal, or belong to a family of Communists, determined to infiltrate the organization. In fact, one mountie's intended wife had a Communist father. But she had already shown her disapproval of his political views. The mountie was allowed to marry her, although after the marriage they were immediately transferred.

"Hey, Kelly! I'm investigating your girlfriend!" Sergeant Reg Irvine poked Bill in the ribs.

Apparently my sins of commission and omission were not discovered, or else they didn't count. Several weeks later, permission granted!

Although by mid-June 1940, Bill's work demanded almost all his time, he came with me to choose furniture and to look at apartments. We rented a pleasant apartment at the corner of Homewood Avenue and Carleton Street, just across from Allen Gardens, at thirty-five dollars a month. Bill also found time to get a marriage license. I suggested a civil ceremony, but agreed to a religious one.

Toward the end of June, Bill asked for three weeks' leave "to get married". Sergeant Veitch relayed the request to Superintendent Schutz, the OC of the CIB.

Soon the sergeant was back, repeating the exact words of the superintendent's response.

"My God!" the superintendent had exclaimed. "He can't have three weeks' leave just to get married! Leave it with me."

"What a rotten outfit I'm in," Bill snapped.

As for me, I felt more strongly than ever that it shouldn't be anybody's business but ours whether we were married or not. Meanwhile, my mother had come from North Battleford at the end of her school year. On July 1 she and I moved into 1 Homewood Avenue, gloomily wondering if Bill and I would ever occupy the place.

Then, on the morning of July 6, a Saturday but a regular RCMP workday, Superintendent Schultz called Bill into his office.

"How much time do you need to get married, Kelly?" he asked.

"I don't need any time off, sir," the would-be bridegroom replied sharply, dangerously close to insubordination. "I can get married any evening sir."

"Oh, no! Don't take it so hard!" Schutz tried to calm his agitated constable. "What about three days?"

"Fine, sir!" Left turn! Quick march out of the OC's office, in accord with RCMP protocol.

Bill spent that day and the next two, Sunday and Monday, finishing urgent work and typing reports. We scheduled his first free day, July 9, for making preparations for our wedding on July 10. July 11 would give us a one-day honeymoon.

On the morning of July 9, Bill, my mother and I enthusiastically unpacked boxes and set everything in place in our top-floor apartment. We stopped occasionally in the spacious living room to admire the effect of the green and rust rug, the green chesterfield and matching chair, and the walnut Nordheimer. In the adjoining dinette our walnut Duncan Fyfe table and matching chairs gleamed in the brightness of the south window. When I spread my peddler girl's lace cloth on the table, we stopped and admired everything all over again.

Unfortunately, as we prepared to hang our few pictures we noticed that the walls were very dirty. The three of us spent several hours washing the walls and woodwork. By the time that Bill and I tackled the bathroom, it was midafternoon. We tried in vain to scrub the thick coating of city grime from the walls, first with soap and water, then with a mild scouring powder, then with the strongest one we could buy from the nearest store. In late afternoon the caretaker gave us some tri-sodium-phosphate, which worked like a charm. We finished the cleaning while my mother prepared a late evening meal.

"Which church are we going to tomorrow?" Mom asked as the three of us did the dishes in the tiny kitchenette.

"Good God!" Bill gasped. "We haven't got a church! Or a minister!"

It seems incredible that we had overlooked them. But nothing was normal in those days. In any case, Bill had done everything that seemed necessary. And as I look back over the years, I think perhaps I had believed we never would be married, and had withdrawn from reality.

About eight that evening Bill and I hurried to nearby Bloor Street, where we had seen several churches but hadn't attended any. Bill planned to track down a minister by way of the notice boards. But the first churches we reached were in darkness. No minister's name was in sight, and there were signs saying "Closed for the summer". Only my faith in Bill's investigative ability kept me from panicking.

About nine o'clock we came to a church with a light shining in the adjoining church hall. No one answered Bill's insistent knocking on the hall door. He climbed on a big wooden box near the window and peered in.

"There's a man on his knees, packing books into boxes," he called down to me. Then, "Hey, you down there!"

"What can I do for you?" the man called back.

"My fiancée and I want to get married tomorrow," Bill shouted.

"We're looking for a minister."

"You're in luck," the man replied. "I'm one." He was packing in readiness to leave for summer camp early next morning, but he would stay long enough to marry us.

No doubt we would have arrived at the church with my mother as our only witness, except that the Reverend Mr. Lapp said we needed two. So we hurried to the apartment of my best friend, Dot White, a young nurse who was also waiting to be married to a mountie. Fortunately, Dot was at home. She signed herself off the next day's duty.

Our wedding party of four assembled at the church hall of Bloor Street United at ten o'clock on the morning of July 10, 1940, the day on which Hitler had over-confidently predicted he would give a garden party at Buckingham Palace. We'd had no time for flowers, of course. But I had a new beige dress chosen, with Bill's approval, far ahead of time at Eaton's, and a wide-brimmed beige straw hat. Bill wore a new light-gray suit with fine white stripes, chosen with my help at Tip-Top Tailors. My mother looked charming in blue, as she always did, and Dot wore her prettiest summer dress, looking refreshingly dainty as usual. After the ceremony the four of us, plus Dot's fiancé, Constable Terry Guernsey, lunched downtown at Simpson's Acadian Court. And that was that!

Later that afternoon, Bill and I escorted my mother to hospital for a pre-arranged foot operation she would have the next day. Then we hurried back to our new home and the pleasure of a twosome supper there.

That night, like Samuel Pepys, "and so to bed". There we relished the thrill of sleeping in our own bed rather than the police beds and others we had shared over the years. To be precise though, the bed wasn't ours. It was a pull-down, push-up Murphy bed built into one wall of the living room. No matter! We considered it ours. Moreover, although the apartment had no bedroom, the wall containing the Murphy bed concealed a dressing room big enough to hold our five dollars worth of furniture, with plenty of space and privacy for the davenport to serve as a single bed when my mother came out of hospital.

As we lay in our own bed that night, smugly content in having at last publicly and respectably declared that we would love and cherish and so on till death us do part, we found living and loving more amazingly satisfying than ever.

It seems anticlimactic to report that we spent our honeymoon the next day by visiting my mother in hospital, then going to a movie. Still, the movie was appropriate: Cary Grant in *My Favourite Husband*.

THIRTEEN

When at last we had achieved marriage, the RCMP began paying Bill a bigger living allowance. Before July 10 he had earned $2.25 a day as a First Class Constable with at least five years' service, plus twenty-five cents a day as a CIB plainclothes allowance. He had also been receiving a living allowance of one dollar a day. Now the Force recognized his married status and added sixty cents a day, which worked out to a wife's food allowance of twenty cents a meal.

RCMP pay was low even for those days, and our milk delivery man earned much more than Bill. But in 1940 we could buy a quart of milk for six cents, and a pound of sausage for twenty. And, as I had worked out a strict budget, we did well on Bill's $4.10 a day. We had all necessities, plus savings, plus entertainment that included a series of five winter concerts by renowned performers at Eaton Auditorium at four dollars a series. Bill also had various other allowances, including some clothing and an annual issue of towels: "bath, 1; hand, linen, 2", as when he was a bachelor.

It seemed strange that Bill's salary was calculated on pay and allowances. Later, however, as I studied the history of the Force, I learned that the system had originated from necessity more than sixty years earlier. In 1874, fewer than 300 original members of the North-West Mounted Police marched more than 800 miles from Manitoba to the vast unsettled Canadian prairies, where they were responsible for policing about 300,000 square miles. At first the federal government had to provide them with pay plus food and clothing. Later, as settlers moved in and settlements were established, the earlier system became pay and allowances, in which the allowances were either in goods or in cash.

In 1940 the system was still in effect. If at the time of our marriage we had been living in married quarters in an "ideal" Saskatchewan detachment such as Bill had promised me at Maidstone, we'd have had free use of all sorts of things. They would have included: "cans, garbage and ash; stoves, heating; stoves, cooking; pipes and elbows, stove; scuttles, galvanized iron or japanned" and so on. Then I, like Tena, would have been expected to use any or all of them while my mountie husband was away on duty.

Fortunately, we were enjoying a comfortable fourth (top) floor apartment with an elevator, an electric stove, hot water heating, and a garbage chute a few steps along the hall. As for laundry, I had no need of the Force's "tubs, wash, galvanized". All our laundry, except Bill's socks and my personal things, went each week to a commercial firm. The friendly driver had shown me how to roll items so tightly that I could get an amazing amount in the big bag provided by the company. Shirts, sheets, pillowcases, towels, and even handkerchiefs and Bill's underwear came back beautifully ironed, all for a dollar a bag. As for the socks and my things, I washed them by hand in convenient tubs in the basement.

Unfortunately, the apartment had a serious drawback: noise, something I had not considered, as I had never before lived in a noisy place. After my mother returned to North Battleford, and I was alone all day and most evenings, the noise seemed worse. I shrank from the constant daytime rush of cars and trucks along Carleton Street, the squealing of brakes at the Homewood Avenue stop sign, and the clanging of streetcars that rattled along Carleton Street every few minutes. Moreover, the night noises kept me from sleeping. I was determined to get used to all outdoor noise, but my unusually acute hearing was my downfall. I was trapped. I felt like a caged animal undergoing experiments to find my breaking point.

Bill, meanwhile, was busy day and night, but he still managed to crowd in several singing lessons a week. By nighttime he was so exhausted that he slept soundly in spite of the noise.

I sometimes crept quietly out of the Murphy bed, dressed in the dark and walked across Carleton Street to Allen Gardens. There I sat on a park bench for part of the night, sometimes weeping uncontrollably. It was noisy in the Gardens, too, but out in the open I didn't feel so unbearably trapped. As the night wore on and the traffic lessened, I regained control of myself and went back to bed, where

Bill was still sound asleep. There I found comfort in remembering that he was safe at home in Canada instead of being overseas and in danger. I must bear the pain of the noise and be thankful. After the war, Bill's singing career would set me free.

As the war progressed, Bill travelled ceaselessly over western Ontario ("O" Division"), revelling in his interesting work. He proved it was not a saboteur, but disgruntled Indians who had put sugar in the engines of federally owned motor boats on Georgian Bay. He discovered who had stolen binoculars donated to the army by patriotic citizens. He found out which one of the thousands of soldiers at Stanley Barracks, near the Toronto exhibition grounds, was stealing money from other soldiers.

His most shocking case that year concerned the National Steel Car Company at Malton. It was making Lancaster bombers, so vitally needed by Britain and her allies. Even so, Royal Canadian Air Force inspectors had reported that men employed at the plant were merely filling in time.

Bill's investigation, of one day only, uncovered an abominable situation. Men in the work centre and in the crowded washrooms sat or stood idle. Only one sound indicated that someone was working. It was made by a man sitting on a platform in a corner, swinging his legs and tapping haphazardly with a wrench against the side of a partly built bomber. Bill also learned that the National Steel Car Company had obtained its government contract on a cost-plus basis. The longer it took to produce a bomber, the more money the company made. After Bill reported the situation, he heard no more about it, but he presumed that the company began producing Lancasters a lot faster.

My mountie husband was always eager to tell me the details of his work, and I was as eager to hear them. Just as I had first admired his youthful ability to police 4,000 square miles, I now admired his ability to perform well in a completely new environment.

Apparently his superiors also appreciated that ability. Although not many plainclothes men became detectives, in November 1940 Bill was promoted to detective rank. As Detective Constable Kelly he received fifty cents a day detective pay, but no plainclothes pay. I adjusted my budget accordingly.

Perhaps Bill's surprisingly early promotion came about because his superiors knew something I knew only later – that his devotion to work went far beyond the normal call of duty. I did catch a glimpse of it, though, at the 1940 RCMP Christmas concert, only five months after our marriage. During the concert, at which Bill sang and I accompanied him, he sat with me. But the moment the concert ended, he dashed away, leaving me alone among scores of strange women and children. He spent the rest of the afternoon discussing cases with fellow mounties who had similarly deserted their wives. It hurt me that on one of our very few social outings, especially one at which the Mounted Police were the hosts, the topic of work took precedence over politeness and sociability.

Even before then I had become unhappy about Bill's singing lessons, although by October 1940 his rich baritone voice had developed into a glorious tenor.

"My God!" one of Mr. M.'s pupils exclaimed after waiting in the hall and then seeing Bill emerge from the studio. "I swear to God I thought it was Jussi Beurling in there!"

I, too, was amazed at the splendid quality of Bill's tenor voice. But I knew that if he aimed at becoming a professional singer, he must learn much more than how to produce his voice. He needed to know at least rudimentary theory, form and harmony, to be able to read music fluently and, preferably, to play the piano. We did a bit of sight reading occasionally, but otherwise Bill used all his limited spare time for doing voice exercises and learning exercise songs. I knew he hadn't time for everything, but it upset me that he couldn't understand my attitude either about his musical needs or about his singing teacher.

One evening soon after we were married, Mr. M. had dinner with us. He declared at great length that his system of voice production was infinitely superior to that of the Conservatory teachers. But they had influence, and could get their students on radio and on concert platforms. Then he suggested that they were not interested in music for art's sake, as he was, but only for money.

I disliked Mr. M.'s attitude toward the Conservatory teachers. Moreover, I couldn't believe that he alone had the key to good voice production. Then I discovered a book used as a text by singing teachers, and I gave the book to Bill. It described Mr. M.'s system exactly, and was entitled *The Caruso Method of Voice Production*. Bill's response was noncommittal.

In the fall Mr. M. began having his pupils give recitals in various homes. At the first one I saw that his method of voice production had not helped many of his pupils.

Fragile little Miss E., – "Well over seventy," my neighbour whispered – followed her singing master's gestures with worshipful gaze as he accompanied her at the piano, conducting with nods. Her wrinkled face and dyed-red hair contrasted strangely with the message of young love that she sang in her thin, shaky voice, but obviously she meant every word of it.

The chubby little Italian boy's voice broke from time to time, which was normal for his age, but which indicated that perhaps it should have been allowed to rest for a time. Of the nine or ten other pupils, one middle-aged woman sang a simple Brahms' song like an operatic aria, complete with exaggerated gestures. Another woman had an uncontrollable vibrato, and another made faces as she strained for high notes she couldn't quite reach. Most of the others did reasonably well, and one woman with obvious musical talent gave a splendid performance.

Bill was the showpiece. At the end of the recital Mr. M. encouraged his frankly adoring pupils by exhibiting Bill as a shining example of his unique method of teaching.

After that, Mr. M. gave Bill operatic arias to learn. They made a great impression at recitals, but they were difficult, and took hours of work by both of us. In vain I begged Bill to take fewer lessons and to learn fewer arias, and to spend time acquiring a musical background.

"You're jealous of M.," he accused me sharply.

I didn't reply. I was indeed jealous, jealous of M.'s influence. But there was no point in explaining again.

At one recital I asked M., privately, to back my requests to Bill.

"No! No!" he exclaimed. "He mustn't miss any lessons. He can get the theory any time. It's not important now."

I began to regard my music with Bill as merely repetitious. Moreover, I didn't even have the satisfaction of accompanying him in public. M. always accompanied his pupils, and Bill refused to ask M. if I might accompany him at the recitals, which by then were our only form of social activity. When I suggested I should ask M., Bill made a fuss. So I spent hours accompanying vocal exercises and helping Bill learn songs and arias, after which he performed beautifully. Then Bill and his maestro took the bows.

"You must be very proud of your husband," one woman whispered. "He's so clever!"

If admiration equalled pride, then certainly I felt it for Bill, not only for his vocal excellence, but also for the splendid police work he continued to do with zeal. But I, too, wanted to be recognized as a worthy individual. I knew that my musical knowledge and skills exceeded those of all the others at the recitals, including M., but my talents were hidden. Perhaps the fact that I never received one word of praise took me back, unconsciously, to my youthful feelings of inferiority. I knew I wasn't inferior in music, but I could see that the others regarded me as such. Perhaps my deep memories of the injustice of male domination simmered below the surface of conscious thought. In any case, I felt that Mr. M. and Bill were conspiring to keep me in a subordinate position. As month followed month and recital followed recital, I became more and more unhappy.

On the other hand, I was lucky in many ways, especially, and in spite of disagreements, in my marriage partnership. Bill and I still loved each other wholeheartedly. Except for anything to do with Bill's maestro, each of us tried to please the other whenever possible, mentally and physically. I aimed to be the best wife I could be, and Bill was intent on giving more to our relationship than he received. In fact, he couldn't have been a better husband, even if Superintendent Schutz had actually lectured him according to RCMP Rules and Regulations on the desirable attitude of a mountie husband, and if Bill had taken all the official advice to heart.

I was also lucky concerning my back, which had improved remarkably, although it would never be normal. I still found pleasure in my friendship with Dot, now Mrs. Terry Guernsey. I patronized the main public library, went to lectures and movies, practiced the piano, and typed odds and ends about my experiences in Toronto. In fact, although my pleasures were mostly solitary, I enjoyed living. Even the traffic noises were not so nerve-racking since winter weather had allowed me to keep the windows closed.

My faith that Bill and I would make a living through music, however, was fading. Unless the war ended soon, so that Bill had time for acquiring a musical background, he couldn't hope to become a professional singer.

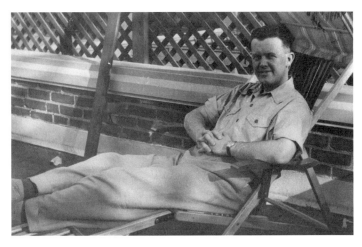

*Summer, 1941. Bill relaxing on the roof at
1 Homewood Avenue.*

1940, Toronto. Bill and I are wearing our wedding clothes as we pose for a snapshot in High Park.

My mother dressed for the wedding.

Summer, 1941, Toronto. I am relaxing on the flat roof of 1 Homewood Avenue.

FOURTEEN

Early in March 1941 the RCMP notified their Detective Constable Reg. No. 12001 that in the middle of the month he would go to "N" (Training) Division at Rockcliffe, Ontario, on the outskirts of Ottawa. There he would attend a three-month class at the Canadian Police College.

I thought of what Tena would have said if she had known that during the first twelve months of our married life Bill would be away for three of them. Fortunately for me, unlike Tena, I was living in a stimulating city, and I had no baby Peggy to keep me housebound. Instead of moping I would expand my horizon.

Bill left for Rockcliffe on a Sunday afternoon. That evening I walked a few blocks to hear a lecture at the Philosophical Society and to begin learning about various religions. In spite of my skeptical attitude toward Christianity, I longed to find a belief in which I could share. The first lecture, on Spiritualism, didn't persuade me, but it gave such vivid descriptions of spiritualist experiences that the only way I could risk falling asleep that night was with all the lights on. I went each Sunday after that, and also studied books from the society's extensive library. However, I didn't find a religion suitable for me.

In any case, lectures and books didn't provide me with the human companionship I needed. In spite of my distrust of Mr. M., I signed up for a series of singing lessons with the class he had just formed. They would give extra tuition to six or seven women among his private pupils. I believed I would fit in well. I had a reasonably pleasant voice, and from my teens I had taken part in school choruses and in musical plays, once in a principal part. And of course I could sight-read music as easily as print. I expected to learn something, to enjoy the companionship of the class, and to be regarded as an individual, not merely as Bill's wife.

It didn't work out that way with the maestro. At the first lesson he asked us to memorize as many of the Italian songs as possible from the book used by all his private pupils. We were to report back at the next week's lesson.

As I had played some of the songs for Bill, and as I was alone and had a week to concentrate on the assignment, I was able to memorize the whole book. I anticipated at least a few words of acknowledgement, but there were none. Looking back, I recognize the same feeling of rejection I'd had as a child, when even 100 per cent on an examination failed to elicit praise from my mother. Mr. M. made me feel even worse by praising the minimal memory work of the vibrato woman. I knew that she painted competently in oils, and that she sold her paintings to pay for two private lessons a week, a number surpassed only by Bill. That thought might have been some consolation for me, but I didn't think of it at the time.

After my first few class lessons, Mr. M. asked me why I didn't take private lessons. I explained that we couldn't afford them. Then he suggested that I might get the money for such lessons by teaching theory to Miss G., one of his private pupils.

"Why don't you give her a free lesson to get her interested?" he asked.

When I gave Miss G. the free lesson, she told me that she didn't like music. She took singing lessons only to please her favourite uncle, who paid for them. She didn't want to study theory or to use more of his money in the process.

"But Mr. M. has arranged with my uncle that you will give me theory lessons, which he says are very necessary," she said. "Then my uncle will pay Mr. M. instead of you, and Mr. M. will give you private lessons for the value of the money he receives."

I was shocked. What a trick! I would never have imagined that even M. would be so devious. According to him, theory was necessary for Miss G., who didn't even want to sing. Yet it was not important for Bill, who hoped for a singing career. Of course Bill would have had to miss a few singing lessons lucrative for M. It would also be lucrative for M. if I gave Miss G. theory lessons for which not I, but he would collect the money.

"Since you don't even like music," I said to Miss G., "you'd be foolish to take theory lessons."

She accepted my advice with obvious relief, and we had a cup of tea to end our first and only theory lesson.

When Mr. M. realized that I was not going to take private lessons, and that I was going to limit my class lessons to one series only, he began asking me to play the piano while the others sang. I did so, wanting nothing more to do with his lessons.

In spite of all my activities, as the warmth of spring demanded open windows, the traffic noises again became unbearable. As before, I resented being trapped, alone, in a cacophony of shrieking brakes, roaring trucks and clanging street cars.

Two sympathetic apartment neighbours advised me to move. They would have moved long ago, except that they liked the apartment and its location. Besides, they were business women, out all day.

The friendly concern of a young woman living just across the hall from me touched me deeply. She was dying of cancer, and was allowed to be free of heavy sedation for only a few hours each day. Her fiancé was with her most of that time, and during a deafening thunderstorm she sent him to knock on my door.

"Miss V. wants to know if you are afraid of thunderstorms," he said. "If so, she wants me to tell you how to make ear stopples to cut out the sound. She uses them herself."

I confessed my distress not only during thunderstorms, but also from the constant traffic noises. Miss V.'s fiancé told me how to make ear stopples, not common in those days, from parawax and cotton batting. In spite of the lump in my throat and the tears welling in my eyes, I tried, but ineffectively, to express my gratitude to Miss V. Then her fiancé hurried back across the hall to report to his dying beloved.

Miss V.'s ear stopples were hard and uncomfortable, and after a few hours I had to remove them. But they gave me periods of blissful relief, and I was thankful.

Bill's few weekend visits brought me further relief. Unlike Tena's husband, Bill was within convenient railway distance of home. Although he spent nearly all his time studying his class lecture notes, at least he was at home, near enough to take me in his loving arms occasionally. And because he needed quiet for study he, too, found the noise objectionable, and thus he understood my distress.

"After our year's lease expires," he promised, "we'll renew it from month to month, and find another apartment."

In turn I developed a more sympathetic understanding of Bill's fascination with and loyalty to the RCMP. Curious as always, I read all his notes. And although I continued to regard the Force as over-bearing, the more I learned about it, the more I admired it.

The RCMP was, in fact, becoming the kind of organization that Commissioner (later Sir) James MacBrien had envisioned when he took office in 1931. It was developing into a modern police force capable of fighting modern criminals with modern methods. Bill and his classmates were taking courses in such scientific subjects as fingerprinting, glass fractures, photography, plan drawing, plaster casts, ballistics, forensic chemistry, and how to track criminals according to their methods of operation (modus operandi).

Bill and the others were learning that the Force's scientific laboratories at Regina and Rockcliffe were among the best-equipped in the world. Laboratory experts could read writing in invisible ink or on burned paper, pick out bloodstains on a handkerchief that looked pure white, do hair analysis, and tell which bullet was shot from which gun. They could slice sections of hair and body tissue infinitesimally thin, magnify photographs up to many hundreds of diameters more than most laboratories of that time could do, and perform scores of other services invaluable to Mounted Policemen out in the field.

In those days such things came as novel ideas, even to most policemen, and they impressed me beyond words. As I learned later, MacBrien's modernization was a far cry from the early days. Then a constable of the original NWMP explained to a disgruntled prisoner what his authority was for arresting him.

"We make up the law as we go along," the constable said.

On July 6, 1941, a few weeks after Bill returned from the Police College, and exactly eight years since he joined the Force, he learned that he had come first in his class. I was less surprised than Bill, but both of us were jubilant.

We scarcely had time to enjoy his triumph, however, or to take note of our first wedding anniversary on July 10. Almost at once he began working on one of the most important RCMP cases of the whole war.

The case involved gold, so necessary during the war. Miners and mill workers in northern Ontario mines were stealing high-grade gold, and a gang of criminals was smuggling it into the United States. The theft was a provincial matter, but the prevention of smuggling was the responsibility of the federal government, and hence of the Mounted Police.

Solving the case was important in two ways. One, the federal government lost money from the nonpayment of taxes on the profits the miners would have made on the stolen gold. Two, because the smugglers feared they could be traced if they cashed large amounts of American money, they received the payment in Canadian funds. This denied the federal government the use of the foreign exchange it should have had in American funds, which the government needed for buying war supplies in the United States. The estimated loss of $1,000,000 in foreign exchange would have bought a lot of vitally necessary supplies.

Investigators of the Foreign Exchange Control Board (FECB) and the RCMP had been working on the case since 1940. They had suspicions, but no proof. So in July 1941 Superintendent Schutz assigned Bill, fresh from the Police College, to the case. He would work with Constable Ted McElhone who was in charge.

As it turned out, it was not the use of modern scientific methods that was needed for the investigation, but mostly old-fashioned leg work, patience and dogged determination. For the next three months Bill, McElhone and two FECB members spent wearisome days and nights watching places and tailing suspects. At first all four took part, but later Bill and Ted took over most of the work.

Bill was scarcely ever at home except to sleep, and sometimes not even then. On his exceptional evenings or Sundays at home, he constantly checked the situation by telephone, or sat waiting for a call.

On the rarest evenings of all, the social ones, either we visited Ted McElhone and his wife, Eileen, or they visited us. Eileen and I wore our prettiest dresses, and prepared delicious refreshments. But invariably and ceaselessly, the men discussed The Gold Case, reliving it and pondering future strategy, even during refreshments. Meanwhile Eileen and I socialized without them and made half-hearted jokes about our husbands' single-minded devotion to duty.

By mid-October, after further slogging and much clever police work, the case was solved. High-graders, middle persons (the main one a woman), and smugglers were arrested, and would be brought to trial later. Newspapers carried column after column of detailed reports, and my BILL scrapbook plumped out considerably.

FIFTEEN

As I tried to reason out what had held Bill so enthralled during the gold case investigation, I decided it must be the thrill of solving a complicated puzzle. Decades later, however, I heard a psychologist discuss the motivation of policemen. He likened police pursuing criminals to ancient hunters pursuing animals.

"Needs have changed over the intervening thousands of years," he said, "but the hunting instinct still survives in the males of our species."

Although I failed to reason correctly as to what drove my mountie husband during the gold case, by the end of the investigation I had learned something important about myself. I realized that I must not continue to fill in time just waiting for Bill to be free to share my life. I must try to achieve a meaningful life of my own.

My lingering back problem limited my choice of occupation. I had been knitting scarves for soldiers and rolling bandages since my marriage, but when I joined a group of women making quilts for the homeless, I couldn't bend in comfort over the quilting frame, and had to give up. I would continue to knit scarves and roll bandages, but I needed more than that.

My two main talents centred on music and words. I immediately ruled out music, in which I could aim only at composition. In those days, even eminent Canadian composers like Dr. Willan complained that it was impossible to have their music performed in public as often as it deserved. As for my writing more songs for Bill, he had no time to learn those I had already written for him. My secondary talent, an ability to use words reasonably well, must sustain me. After we moved to a quiet apartment I would develop that talent.

On October 1 we moved to number 27 on the quiet residential Winchester Street. Our apartment was one of four in a substantial brick building. The tenants of the other apartments, all adults, were out all day, so I was living in a quiet apartment on a quiet street. Halleluia!

Our apartment had disadvantages, but I didn't care: it was quiet. The living room was exactly the same size as our nine-foot by twelve-foot rug. On it sat the piano, piano bench, chesterfield, big chair, hassock, bookcase, two dining chairs and two end tables. The Duncan Fyfe table, its leaves dropped, sat out in the small entrance hall, and so did the other two dining chairs. The telephone was also in the hall, but hanging on the wall, presumably to save space. There was a big bedroom, though, so we bought a handsome limed-oak bedroom suite, and at last we owned our own bed. Then we put nearly all the rest of our belongings in the bedroom, which still was not overcrowded.

The kitchen was small, but held our "Property-of-Such-and-Such-Parish-Church-Hall" table and chairs as well as a small refrigerator and a small gas stove. The stove went with the apartment, but I was afraid of gas leaks and explosions. So, with the permission of the understanding owner, we had it taken out, and we bought a small plug-in electric stove.

On that stove I, the cook, could use at any one time, either the two top elements, or the top and bottom oven elements, or one of each. After a while I got used to juggling the heat for producing commendable meals, but by Thanksgiving I hadn't worked out the most suitable combinations. So for our Thanksgiving dinner, at which I was indeed truly thankful, we had weiners heated on one top element, cold wiener buns, tea made from water heated on the other top element, and fruit salad. We ate at the kitchen table, the only usable one. But we merely laughed and toasted each other with hot tea.

Our new home had no laundry facility for tenants, but I was still using the dollar-a-bag system, and it was easy to wash Bill's socks in the bathroom handbasin. As for my personal things, I washed them in the bathtub. To avoid too much bending I stepped barefoot into the tub and trod the clothes as if I were treading grapes to make wine. I rinsed them the same way. In spite of the inconvenience, I was happy. And so, therefore, was Bill.

Soon after Thanksgiving I went to the first lecture of the journalism class given as an extension course that fall by the University of Toronto.

Harriet Parsons' introductory lecture invigorated me. The next day, using my portable typewriter on the kitchen table, I wrote to the School Publications Company that had published my book of songs. I asked if they would like a little book of poems that could be used as recitations in primary grades. Editor Belva Howatt replied that she would. I set to work at once, lying in bed to write the poems (mere verses really!) in longhand, then typing them at the kitchen table.

At the second journalism class Miss Parsons gave us an assignment: "Write up to 1,500 words about something you know."

I wrote about teaching at Brightsand Lake School in rural Saskatchewan, where on my first teaching day the children and I cleaned out a battered old foot-pumped parlour organ. The big boys removed a nest of newborn mice, and helped me mend the canvas straps on the pedals. Then, with organ accompaniment, we all sang "God Save the King", because that was the only song those music-deprived children knew. I didn't write about patriarch-trustee Alonzo S., but I did write about his thirteen-year-old daughter Grace. In winter, on her own initiative, she organized vegetable contributions from every family represented by the children. Then she made soup, mostly turnip, on the wood-burning pot-bellied heater. Thus the children, many of whom brought only bread and jam in their lard pails for lunch, had extra nourishment and warmth.

In my assignment I also wrote of other things that still touched me emotionally. I told about six-year-old Ray, for whom I made a winter coat from his father's overcoat, and how Ray showed his gratitude by using the scraps to make me a pair of strange-looking mittens.

I wrote of the two Grade 8 boys, Wilfred and Ralph, who understood why I hadn't been able to cover everything set out in the school curriculum for Grade 8. They could see that I was also struggling to teach more than twenty other pupils in seven other grades. As the boys' very important provincially-marked final exams approached, at their own request, they came to school on Saturdays so that we could cover what I'd been unable to cover during the year. Wilfred and Ralph also vied for the privilege of unsaddling my horse each morning, feeding it at noon, and resaddling it after school.

There were so many things I could tell about my teaching in "The Little White Schoolhouse", as I titled my assignment. I used the whole 1,500-word allowance.

Two weeks later Harriet Parsons returned our assignments. She thought mine was saleable, and suggested a possible market. I could hardly wait to send it out, and to get started on the next assignment: "Write about something else you know."

"I know a lot about the RCMP," I said to Bill. "I think I'll write about that."

"Oh, no, you won't!" Bill exclaimed. "I won't have you writing about anything to do with my work."

I didn't argue. Bill had made a fuss when he knew I intended to write the article about Dale. But I wrote it, and *Maclean's* published it, and there was no harm done. Now I would write something about the RCMP, even if it turned out to be only for practice.

A few days later, on November 17, we were astonished to learn that Bill had been promoted to the rank of corporal. Actually, his promotion was to an acting rank, with the understanding, as was normal, that after a year of satisfactory service, the rank would be confirmed as permanent.

As corporal, Bill would receive more basic pay, and an extra twenty cents a day for what I considered a wife's living allowance. Also, as a detective corporal he would receive seventy-five-cents-a-day detective pay, but no plainclothes allowance.

The first full month at the new rate of pay was, of course, December. My records show that during that month we paid a sixteen-dollar installment on two War Savings Certificates, plus the cost of Christmas gifts and festive luxury foods. In addition there were the normal expenses – food, shelter, clothing, stamps at three cents each, newspapers at three cents each, street car tickets at three for twenty-five cents, and so on. At the end of the month we had one dollar left in spite of Christmas expenses. We must have felt affluent. The following month Bill had a new suit, paid for in cash as were all our purchases, so that my accounts would always be in order.

Meanwhile, Bill and I realized that the most important thing about his promotion was that it had come so unusually early in his service. Secretly I was disturbed as I remembered that before Bill had thought of turning to singing, he had hoped eventually to become a sergeant. This second early promotion indicated that he would certainly become a sergeant if he stayed with the Force.

Uneasily I wondered if he might now be influenced to change his mind about a singing career. The possibility worried me. I didn't ask Bill about it, though, for fear of hearing what I didn't want to hear. As it was, the thought of staying with the Force kept nagging me. Nagging, nagging, nagging.

SIXTEEN

Bill's promotion to corporal made no difference to his work. Neither did the end of the gold case investigation, although I had expected he would be less busy after that. Now, however, he and Ted McElhone worked ceaselessly, preparing for the trials by organizing the mass of evidence that involved 80 witnesses and 150 exhibits.

Even so, Bill managed to squeeze in singing lessons. He made up for the half-hour lessons he had missed during his police college and gold case days by extending lesson periods to an hour and even, occasionally, to an hour and a half, again fitting them in whenever he found time. That indicated to me that he still hoped for a singing career. Thus my fears were allayed, at least for the time being, that he would stay with the Force. Then, in spite of the disadvantages at 27 Winchester Street, I settled in happily.

While I lay on the bed writing my book of recitations in longhand, or typing them at the kitchen table, I ignored the surroundings as I did what I enjoyed. Besides, for the first time since I stopped teaching, I felt the pleasure of being close to children, whoever they might be, who would enjoy my work just as my own pupils had done.

I also completed the second journalism assignment. It was an article about the training of RCMP dogs like Dale of Cawsalta: "Police Dogs Go to School".

"Excellent," Miss Parsons said when she returned it in mid-December, "and probably saleable."

"That's what she thinks!" Bill exclaimed when I got home that night, thrilled at the praise. "As far as I'm concerned, it's not saleable, and neither is anything else you write about my work!"

It seemed strange that my life was controlled by the Force, and that I was learning more and more about it and even admiring it, yet I wasn't allowed to report what I was learning. Newspaper and magazine writers, by contrast, told what they knew, and sometimes what they thought they knew but didn't. I decided to send the article out anyway.

Two days later, exactly a month after Bill was promoted to the rank of corporal, I went as a spectator to the Supreme Court of Ontario, where Bill and Sergeant Veitch were defendants in a civil suit. Miss Sophie K., a strange little middle-aged woman, was asking damages of $10,000 against the two Mounted Policemen. She alleged that they had persecuted her and interfered with her social and business life.

I was well acquainted with the background of the case. Several years earlier, Miss K. had complained to the Toronto CIB that postal officials were interfering with her mail. The CIB found that was not true. Then she pestered Sergeant Veitch by telephone, often for an hour at a time. When Bill went to the CIB in 1939, Veitch passed the case to him. Bill found nothing wrong, and then Miss K. pestered him. Bill learned that Miss K. owned, or thought she owned – he never found out which – a small company called the Royal Canadian Coal Company. She believed that the Royal Canadian Mounted Police were her competition and were disrupting her business.

When she got no satisfaction from Bill, she telephoned Commissioner S.T. Wood in the middle of the night and complained to him. Bill was sent to tell her never to do that again.

"You tell S.T. Wood that I'm a taxpayer and he's a public servant, and I'll call him any time I like!" the irate complainant exclaimed to Bill. He reported to the commissioner accordingly.

Then she decided to sue, and now I sat in court, looking at the woman who was such a nuisance. Her unnaturally brilliant red hair created a bright spot in the drab courtroom. She sat erect, looking ready to strike. On her lap lay an oversized brown paper bag that held the records she carried everywhere, some of which she intended to use against her alleged "persecutors".

As the trial proceeded, it seemed to me that Bill and Sergeant Veitch needed a champion. I knew that Sophie had no lawyer, and that court officials had helped her prepare her case in the proper form. Now I saw that even Mr. Justice McFarlane helped her by sympathetically allowing statements and procedures he never would have allowed a lawyer to use. I could see, too, that Sophie was as cunning as Bill reported. Most of her accusations were so vague that the defendants had no way of disproving them.

I began to worry that the $10,000 would be assessed against the defendants. I knew that the Force had a set policy as to the paying or not paying the cost of defending RCMP members charged in criminal cases. If a mountie lost his case, the Force had no obligation. And I had read that even if an accused mountie was found not guilty, the Force would merely "consider paying" his expenses. Bill didn't know of any RCMP policy concerning civil cases, but I presumed it would be about the same as for criminal cases. Considering that Bill was earning about five dollars a day, and Sergeant Veitch only a few dollars more, it would take the two of them countless years to pay off $10,000.

I was also worried that if we lost the case, we would no doubt also have to pay court costs and the lawyer's fee. Bill and his sergeant, thinking of Sophie's cunning, had hired the top-ranking, high-priced lawyer, T.N. Phelan. They had the approval of the Force and, I believe, of the Minister of Justice, but in view of the Force's set policy regarding criminal trials, I didn't find much comfort in that. Incidentally, Mrs. Veitch and I had also given our approval, signifying that if our husbands lost their case, we were ready to scrimp on household expenses for as many years as necessary.

"Don't worry," Bill had said, trying to comfort me. "If we have to pay, maybe Mr. Phelan won't charge us as much as he would have charged the government."

Even so, as I sat in the courtroom and realized the sympathy being accorded Sophie, I still worried about the $10,000 plus court costs plus Mr. Phelan's fee.

Then at last, fortunately for the Veitches and the Kellys, Sophie made a big mistake. She told the court how Sergeant Veitch, in disguise, had followed her about the streets of Toronto. And at last the lawyer for the defence stepped forward with more confidence.

"You say that Sergeant Veitch, in disguise, followed you, Miss K.?"

"Yes."

"Then how did you recognize him?"

"By the shape of his legs."

"Was Sergeant Veitch in disguise in women's clothing?"

"No."

"Did he have any pants on?"

"Yes."

"Then how did you recognize the shape of his legs?"

No answer.

Case dismissed.

Even then, we four most affected were not free of worry. Miss K. appealed to the Appeal Court of Ontario, asking it to reverse the lower court's decision. On losing that appeal, she asked permission to appeal to the Supreme Court of Canada, the highest court in the land. T.N. Phelan objected that the action was "frivolous and vexatious", but Sophie's appeal was allowed. Perhaps at that point she gave up. In any case, Bill and Sergeant Veitch had no more trouble with Miss Sophie K.

Eventually the RCMP paid the fee of the expensive Mr. Phelan, by way of federal government funds, by way of Canadian taxpayers. It seemed most unfair that one obviously unbalanced person could use the Canadian judicial system to waste so much valuable police time and taxpayers' money. On the other hand, I realized that such situations were part of the price we paid for democracy.

Meanwhile, the Christmas season of 1941 had given Bill a short respite from his around-the-clock work. He sang at the RCMP Christmas concert, where I accompanied him, and where the men again deserted their wives to discuss cases. He also sang at Maestro M.'s Christmas recital, where I did not accompany him.

Our apartment had no room for even the smallest tree, but with my now-skillful manoeuvering on the plug-in stove we celebrated Christmas with a full-course dinner, during which we toasted Detective Corporal Bill.

As corporal, however, he had extra duty every two weeks or so. The NCOs took turns, at night and on weekends and holidays, as Orderly NCO at the Beverley Street barracks. There they took emergency calls, checked the movement of police cars in and out, and so on, and at a late hour were allowed to sleep at the barracks. So Bill spent his first New Year's Day as a corporal on duty downtown.

It was a suitable beginning for the year 1942, which was immediately as busy as any year to date. Not only was Bill working overtime on the evidence of the gold case trials in Canada, but he also made many trips to Buffalo, New York. There he helped United States treasury officials to organize their evidence of the trials of the United States citizens involved in the gold case, and to co-ordinate the Canadian and United States evidence. Also, because of his Police College experience the previous year, he gave lectures after office hours. Some were to members of the Force, and others were to Norwegian Military Police at their base in Gravenhurst, Ontario.

In March of 1942, when gasoline rationing came into effect, his workload increased. Almost at once the Department of Munitions and Supply was inundated with reports from patriotic citizens about violations. Many of them occurred in Toronto, where Bill was designated to investigate. As the number of violations increased, he was put in charge of what came to be known as the black market squad. At first it had only one other member, Constable Barry Graham. But as the war progressed and more substances became scarce, either they were rationed or their use was restricted, and the black market squad sometimes had as many as fifteen members.

Gasoline rationing meant inconvenience for many Canadians, and a loss of income for some. And since the Japanese attack on Pearl Harbour had driven the United States into the war, that country had also established gasoline rationing. Consequently, Canadians no longer had access to gasoline across the border, and thus many of them got gasoline in any illegal way they could.

The offenders must have heard alarming radio reports about the desperate situation concerning gasoline, but they ignored the fact that the substance was vitally important overseas. It took 1,600,000 gallons of gasoline to send a fleet of 1,000 bombers from England on a raid over Berlin, and it took 12,000 gallons to train each pilot. As for gasoline used in Canada, it came in as crude oil transported by tankers. In fact, our rationing started when enemy submarines made the Atlantic waters so dangerous that tankers were being sunk daily.

One of Bill's early gasoline ration cases came up for trial about two weeks after the gold case trials began. I sat in the courtroom and learned how William Glenesk, a 51-year-old employee in a Spadina branch of the Oil Controller's office, had been taking bribes to give gasoline ration applicants higher categories than they were entitled to get.

I heard many fascinating details, but the case was straightforward. Bill had met Glenesk and had posed as a candy salesman who wanted a higher category than the AA category (the lowest) to which he was entitled. For seventy-five dollars Glenesk would accept Bill as a cattle buyer and would give him a D, a much higher category. Bill made out the application, but Glenesk added his occupation as cattle buyer.

Bill arranged the deal so as to have complete proof that would be accepted in court. This included having two plainclothes mounties near enough to see him pass the money, in marked bills, to Glenesk. Then, after the offender had walked far enough away from Bill, the other two mounties searched Glenesk, retrieved the money, and arrested him.

At his trial, Glenesk was found guilty and sentenced to a jail term of two years less a day. Later, charges were laid against others to whom he had illegally issued gasoline ration categories. They in turn went to jail or paid fines.

With keen appreciation of Bill's contribution to the war effort, I pasted several more newspaper clippings in my BILL scrapbook.

By this time Canadians were trafficking in sheets of gasoline ration coupons, and even in individual coupons stolen from ration books. The daily entries in my journal during 1942 indicated Bill's heavier work load as more and more callous citizens disregarded wartime regulations.

Some entries noted that he worked till 9:15 p.m., till 1 a.m., till 2 a.m., all day Sunday, at night, all night, all day Saturday at a conference. My journal also reported: Bill to Dunville; to Barrie overnight; to St. Catharines overnight; to Camp Borden and home at 10 p.m.; to Montreal; to Niagara Falls; and so on. Three successive entries noted: Bill away; Bill still away; Bill back at night. Other entries noted that he also shared such extra work as Orderly NCO and special telephone duty. Still others noted his cancellation of singing lessons again and again, then the fact that Mr. M. had joined the merchant navy.

After that Bill had lessons from Mr. Roselini, whom he had known in Saskatchewan as Mr. Roselyn. His lessons with Mr. Rosselini, like those with Mr. M., sometimes lasted an hour and a half as Bill tried to make up for time lost.

During that hectic period I was thankful that my mountie husband was contributing so constantly to the war effort. I was even more thankful that he was doing it while still safe at home in Canada. Even so, and even though I knew that many wives were enduring much more than I was, I still longed for the time when Bill and I could have a more normal married life.

SEVENTEEN

No matter how busy Bill was during 1942, I was almost as busy in my way as he was in his. To celebrate his raise in pay as a corporal we had bought a Singer sewing machine, one of the last available till after the end of the war. The price included a series of twenty lessons, and I immediately resumed the sewing I had always enjoyed. I felt great satisfaction in creating something worthwhile from very little cash outlay, just as I'd felt when I began sewing at age fifteen. Now I made not only my own clothes, but also clothes for Bill. First came a beige and brown sports jacket, although he had no time for sports. Then I made a handsome deep-green flannel smoking jacket, although he didn't smoke and he had no time to wear that jacket either.

In early April, when Bill had to go to Hamilton, I went with him, by forbidden police car as in our North Battleford-Maidstone days. There I visited Miss Howatt, editor of School Publications, and got orders for booklets of plays, drills, primary concert programs, and odds and ends of songs, stories and recitations for use in Holiday Packages.

I was so exhilarated at receiving so many orders that the next day, back in Toronto, I ordered a custom-made black Persian lamb coat. Then I hurried to fill Miss Howatt's orders so that I could pay for the coat.

I did something else, equally satisfying, but for no payment: I helped eleven-year-old David prove to the Toronto school board that he was not retarded. I had met his mother, a widow like my own mother, when both of us were tenants at 1 Homewood Avenue. When I saw her on a streetcar in the spring of 1942, she looked haggard and hopeless.

"The school board says David is retarded," she murmured. "They're going to put him in an industrial school where he'll only learn to work with his hands."

The problem, she explained, was twofold. For one thing, David was only in Grade 4, two years behind most children his age. Worse still, he couldn't even do Grade 1 arithmetic.

"But he's not retarded," his mother insisted. "He can read the Grade 6 reader."

"Then he certainly isn't retarded," I agreed. "I'll help him with his arithmetic."

So David's mother told the schoolboard that he was being tutored, and his banishment to an industrial school was temporarily suspended.

For many months David came several times a week after school, and on Saturdays. We sat at the table in the cramped little kitchen at 27 Winchester Street. There we began at the beginning, with one plus one, and there we did arithmetic and more arithmetic. Poor David, I learned, had been sick for long periods right from his Grade 1 days. He had missed so much schooling that he'd never had a chance to catch up on what he'd missed. At last his skill in arithmetic equalled his skill in reading. The label "retarded" was withdrawn, and his sentence to the industrial school was commuted. All three of us – David, his mother and I – rejoiced.

Meanwhile, I was less successful in helping myself. No matter how busy I kept myself, and no matter how I enjoyed whatever I did, I ached with longing for Bill's companionship. Granted, during that work-crammed, black market squad period he did his best with what little spare time he had. We went to occasional concerts to hear such notables as tenor Jan Kiepura and pianist Arthur Rubenstein. Sometimes we took a Sunday picnic supper to Riverdale Park. Also, occasionally we went on Sunday to the Toronto Art Gallery or the Royal Ontario Museum. Those highlights, however, couldn't make up for all the suppertimes, the evenings, the whole nights, and the Sundays and holidays I spent alone.

In March Bill had done his best to please me by agreeing that his birthday gift to me would be a series of dancing lessons for both of us, as I loved dancing almost as much as music, and he didn't dance. But almost always he was too busy to attend, so I went alone. I also went alone to Promenade concerts, to lectures where I learned fascinating things I longed to share with Bill, and to movies where I laughed alone and, at *The Oxbow Incident*, which featured a lynching, I wept alone.

As the year wore on, selfish Canadians not only dealt in illegal gasoline ration coupons, but they also produced counterfeit coupons. In fact, there were so many counterfeit coupons on the market that the RCMP Crime Detection Laboratory at Rockcliffe set up a central filing system for the classification and origin of each type as it came into circulation. Under the circumstances, Bill was busier than ever, and my usual composure deserted me. I began to worry that desperate criminals might harm him to prevent their being sent to jail.

One of the worst things for me to endure was waiting, waiting, waiting, not knowing when Bill would come home. During the gold case I had learned that Annie Newman, the main intermediary between the high-graders and the smugglers, was the common-law wife of the notorious Rocco Perri. While he was serving a jail term, she was in charge of his "business" operations. I had heard alarming stories about such gangsters, including the rumours that the body of at least one of their rivals had been dropped into the depths of Lake Ontario, encased in a "cement overcoat". I knew that Detective Corporal Bill didn't carry his revolver because he wore plainclothes, and as I waited for his return, I imagined all sorts of horrible happenings.

One night at eleven o'clock, I had been waiting nervously for five hours, knowing Bill couldn't telephone me that night, but expecting he would be home at any moment. When the wall telephone rang, I was so distraught that I shrieked "Hello" into the mouthpiece. There was no answer, so I never knew who had heard my ear-piercing shriek.

At such times of distress I comforted myself by remembering that whenever Bill had a chance he let me know where he was, and when he hoped to get home. He wasn't at all like his fellow mountie who often worked late with him. Even when Bill set a good example by telephoning me, that constable failed to phone his wife, although she was at home with a new baby.

Nevertheless, my longing for Bill's company, my fears for his safety, and my unbearable anxiety as I waited drove me to bouts of weeping. At first I wept only when I was alone. Later, in the mornings just as Bill was ready to leave, I broke down completely.

"You never should have married a Mounted Policeman," he exclaimed bitterly one morning during my weeping spell.

"Certainly not you," I sobbed. "With someone else I might at least have shared a little home life. Even your men on the black market squad have some time off, but you don't. You don't need me! All you need is work!"

Bill was so upset that he told one of the older men on his squad how unhappy I was.

"Never mind, Bill," Constable G. soothed him. "Even Jesus Christ couldn't please Nora."

For a time, whenever we quarrelled Bill quoted what Constable G. had said about me. After that he used the statement as his own.

We were both so unhappy that I asked Bill to come with me to a marriage counsellor, but he adamantly refused. So I went, alone, to see David's psychologist.

Dr. M. asked me what I did when I was alone. I told him that I wrote, sewed and played the piano. The season was early fall, and the day was unusually chilly, so I was wearing two garments I had made. One was a fully-lined bottle-green wool bouclé suit with special same-colour buttons shaped like snail shells. The other was a brown wool bouclé cape, also lined, and with careful detailing around the armholes. I couldn't take any credit for my small rust-coloured felt hat, but at least it complemented the suit and cape. Dr. M. said he was impressed.

As David's psychologist questioned me further, both of us learned a lot about me, and I saw myself from his impersonal viewpoint. When I left his office I felt more like a worthy individual, better able to cope with whatever I had to cope.

On the way home by streetcar, I realized that my new outlook was already affecting my behaviour. An unusually fat man came and sat beside me. As often happened on Toronto street cars, he slumped down low in the seat and spread his outstretched legs so wide apart that he used the space of more than one seat, crowding me severely. For the first time in my life I defended myself against the attitude of an insensitive male by suddenly jabbing the sprawling leg of this one with my nearest knee. He immediately straightened up and moved into his own space, at which point I felt a small surge of triumph.

During the years that followed my visit to David's psychologist I learned more about myself, and I grew to understand Bill's early frustration with me. But I also learned more about Bill, and in turn I understood him. Many years after he had become an officer, I complained to Lloyd Bingham about Bill's constant work overload. Bingham had been Bill's close friend since their North Battleford days together and he, like Bill, had by then become an officer. Over the years each had followed the details of the other's career.

"It was Bill's own fault that he was overworked," Bingham

snapped, springing to the defence of the Force. "He always chose to do more than anyone else. He could have had free time if he'd wanted it."

It came as a shock to me that Bill sheepishly agreed.

Years later I was even more shocked to learn the specifics of Bill's attitude to his black market work. He probably thought I already knew, or he wouldn't have explained to friends within my hearing about his work as head of the squad. He admitted that he could have stayed in the office, keeping regular hours, while his men made the investigations and did the after-hours work. But Bill found the investigations so fascinating that he undertook as many as possible himself, and this was in addition to doing what would have been full-time office work for anyone else.

"It was great!" he exclaimed. "I'd track down one black marketeer, and he'd lead me to half a dozen others. I couldn't get enough of it." And on another occasion he declared, "It was a policeman's paradise."

Still later he admitted to me that his eagerness to leave Saskatchewan in 1939 came not only from his desire to have a singing career, or even to hasten our marriage. What he wanted as much as anything was to escape from the monotony of rural work and become involved in the more varied work of federal policing.

It was a good thing I didn't know those things during the war years, which were also the first years of our married life. I would have experienced even more stress if I had known that my beloved husband worked incessantly, not because the Force ordered it, although that was sometimes the case, but because he preferred his fascinating work to anything and anyone else.

EIGHTEEN

Although I didn't realize the depth of Bill's obsession with police work during his black market days, I gradually accepted the fact that it was all-embracing. I also accepted the fact that for the sake of my mental health I must disassociate myself from my longing to be what I had grown up believing was normal for women. Because of that widely-accepted norm, I had always expected that after marriage I would develop into a loving, companionable wife, homemaker and mother.

My back problem ruled out the third of that trio. In any case, I had become disenchanted as I saw how miserable some Mounted Police wives were as they raised their children practically alone. As for my being a companionable wife and homemaker, under the circumstances that, too, was beyond me. Certainly the love was there, but obviously it wasn't enough. I must immerse myself in some other useful, companiable occupation.

Soon after my visit to Dr. M., I thought I had found what I needed. In the fall of 1942, after three years of devastating war and with no end in sight, the federal government urged women to help the war effort by becoming draftsmen. Then they would work on plans for war equipment. I remembered my keen pleasure in high school geometry, and with great enthusiasm I signed up for the training program. But after one day of bending over a drafting board, my back went into painful spasm. I withdrew from the program feeling desolate.

I should have known better than to sign on. Even rolling bandages for a full day with nowhere to lie down and relax had been too much for me. I'd had to restrict my war work to what I'd been doing since early in the conflict – knitting scarves for soldiers.

Oh well, I'd keep on knitting scarves, and concentrate on writing. I had sold my "Little White Schoolhouse" article immediately, and since then a few others. I had even helped the war effort with "Save Our Sugar", an SOS article urging people to use less than their ration allowance of sugar. Thus in that way they could, figuratively, throw a sugar bowl at Hitler.

The article explained that sugar could be used to make high-test ethyl alcohol, which in turn was used in aerial bombs, torpedoes and smokeless powder. I noted that every time a sixteen-inch shell was fired it used alcohol from as much sugar as could be produced in one season from one-fifth of an acre of rich Cuban soil.

As for my other writing, when I considered my encouraging beginning with School Publications, it seemed that I could sell as much there as I cared to write.

In mid-October I began my second Toronto University extension course, Authorship. I didn't learn much this time, but the course led to my joining the Pen Guild and forming lasting friendships with three women, just as I had made two special friends during the journalism course. After that we six encouraged one another, and we all thrilled to even the smallest success of any one of us. So now I had congenial friends and encouragement.

About the time the authorship class took its Christmas break I paid, with my own money and with great satisfaction, for my black Persian lamb coat. I even had enough money left to buy Christmas gifts for Bill and my mother.

A few days later, I went with Bill to our third RCMP Christmas concert. It was with even greater satisfaction that I wore that beautiful form-fitting coat. In keeping with the coat I wore a little black pillbox hat trimmed with Persian lamb. Actually, the hat was a markdown bargain from Eaton's basement, but it certainly complemented the coat to perfection. I also wore the smart little black dress I'd finished making only days earlier, and some of the handsome silver jewellery I'd been collecting piece by piece, as birthday and Christmas gifts from Bill and my mother, at my own request.

That ensemble provided me with a protective shield against the attitude of the Force's males. In fact, it provided me with such a sense of security that after the concert when, as usual, Bill and the other mounties deserted their wives for the keen pleasure of discussing their work, I didn't even care what they did.

By January 1943 rubber had become very scarce. Wartime Prices and Trade Board regulations stated that anyone who needed to buy new or reconditioned tires must get a permit. Not all applications were approved. So almost at once some Canadians got tires as they got gasoline, in any illegal way they could.

From mid-January, Bill and his squad were busier than ever. Like many black marketeers, some soldiers at Camp Borden were now dealing in tires as well as in gasoline ration coupons. Again and again I went to police court and was shocked, as in the case of Private Fletcher, who pleaded guilty to seven charges. Magistrate McNish gave him a scathing reprimand and sentenced him to three months on each charge. But, as usual, the sentences were to run concurrently. Thus Fletcher served his twenty-one month sentence in three months. He probably felt that he might as well commit multiple offences as a single one. Many other offenders received similar concurrent sentences. They probably felt the same as Fletcher.

I wondered why magistrates and judges didn't help the war effort by giving more sentences to be served consecutively, at least as a warning to others. That would have been much more of a deterrent than the most scathing reprimand.

Fortunately, the black market squad hadn't much extra work from the rationing of sugar since January 1942, or of tea and coffee since August of that year. Ration allowances of those commodities were so generous that it was not worthwhile for anyone to steal, sell or counterfeit coupons for sugar, tea or coffee. In fact, we had such ample allowances that Bill and I were able to include good amounts of all three in the food parcels we still sent to his parents, then living in severely rationed England. Nevertheless, sugar-bearing ships were still being sunk.

In spite of little extra work from sugar, tea and coffee rationing, the black market squad had plenty to do, week after week, month after month. Entries in my journal from March 23 through March 25 noted: Bill worked till midnight; Bill worked late; Bill worked till 11 p.m. Then on March 26: Bill Orderly NCO. About a week later, on Saturday, April 3: Bill up at 4 a.m. and not home till one o'clock Sunday morning. That same morning, after only five hours rest, he was up at 6 a.m. and out working again.

Meanwhile, although I still retained feelings of inferiority, further sales of my writing somewhat improved my self-image. Also, the companionship of my writing friends allowed me to be more objective in accepting life with a minimum of Bill's company. In any case, I still admired him, still loved him. Even though he was busier than ever, my changed outlook allowed me to be happy. As for Bill, he had always demonstrated his love and concern as time permitted. Now that I was obviously happy, so was he. Life became more pleasant for both of us.

Enthusiastically, we planned to buy a house, and early in April 1943 we found the right one, price $5,500. It was a substantial red brick bungalow at 400 Deloraine Avenue, in North York, just across the northern boundary of the city of Toronto. The following weekend my busy mountie husband made time on Saturday afternoon for us to meet the owner, Mr. Harry Jenkins. We met at the bungalow to discuss details of purchase and to set the date of occupancy as June 1.

Mr. Jenkins was a builder with very high standards. Since retiring from big projects he had built one house at a time, lived in it for two years, then built another, and so on. He was presumably a competent businessman, but he had unusual consideration for others. In fact, getting to know the remarkable Mr. Jenkins gave us back some of the faith we had lost as Bill dealt with more and more Canadians who broke the law in pursuit of their own avaricious aims.

Mr. Jenkins had set the down payment at $1,000, but when he knew that we would have to borrow that amount as a second mortgage, he lowered the down payment to $800. Then he offered to lend it to us at a lower rate of interest than we would otherwise have had to pay. We accepted with astonishment and gratitude.

As we left 400 Deloraine, Bill and I were exhilarated about owning our own house. Enthusiastically, we agreed to live within an even stricter budget to repay our twofold debt. Bill had recently given up his singing lessons because he had absolutely no time for practice. The money we saved in that way would go toward the repayment. Then, with my newly developed self-confidence prompting me, I offered to pay half the down payment from my future earnings. $400 seems a small amount now. But changing money values over the decades make it the equivalent of $4,000 to $5,000, perhaps more, in the late 1990s.

Three days later I showed good intent toward keeping my promise by going to see Miss Jean Browne, the editor of the *Canadian Red Cross Junior* magazine. She asked me to write a children's play. If she liked it, I could write regularly for her. As soon as I got home I began writing a play about Madame Curie. It was the beginning of my monthly writing for the *Canadian Red Cross Junior.*

The following Tuesday I mailed *Madame Curie* to Miss Browne. Then I took the train to Hamilton to see Miss Howatt of School Publications. She gave me three regular orders and an extra one. The latter entailed rewriting a booklet on *How to Cope with a Coping Saw*, which someone else had written for her but which, she said, was unintelligible. I didn't known anything about coping saws, but later I rewrote the booklet in a form that even I, and hence anyone else, could understand. Miss Howatt was delighted.

A few days after my trip to Hamilton the mail brought me a cheque for the RCMP article I'd written as my second journalism assignment. Miss Parsons had praised it, and I had sent it out in spite of Bill's prohibition and without his knowledge. Since it was only about the training of police dogs, and it went only to a Sunday-school paper, I didn't see how Bill could object. As it happened, he didn't object, so I felt free to do other RCMP articles for such innocuous publications.

My happiness at the way things were working out led me to plan a celebration of our house purchase, somehow, over the Easter weekend. It dampened my spirits to learn that Bill would be orderly officer on Good Friday, that he would have to work all day Saturday, and stay at home all Easter Sunday waiting for telephone calls. Then he would have to leave early on Easter Monday morning for Niagara Falls. Nevertheless, I shrugged off my disappointment, and Good Friday morning found me at the kitchen table, typing contentedly.

When the wall telephone rang I presumed it would be one of the usual nuisance calls that so often interrupted my work. I expected that someone was calling with information for Bill that would lead to more work and more time away from home.

Instead it was Bill himself. In great excitement he told me that he had been promoted to sergeant. Again it was a surprise, coming unusually early in his service, and only six months after he had been confirmed as a corporal.

I relished the promotion for Bill's sake, and felt a surge of admiration that he had become a detective sergeant with less than ten years' service. After I replaced the receiver, however, I sank into the nearest chair, weak from the confused thoughts that suddenly surged in my mind. Eventually I found the strength to accept reality: this promotion to sergeant meant that Bill would never leave the Force. Even so, I didn't feel the same anxiety I had felt when he was promoted to corporal. This time I had my writing to sustain me. Besides, in spite of everything we still loved each other. Things would work out somehow.

NINETEEN

Bill's promotion to sergeant not only brought him more seniority, but also an increase in pay and allowances. His detective pay as a sergeant also increased, to one dollar a day. What affluence! And what perfect timing!

We moved into 400 Deloraine Avenue as planned, on June 1. The bungalow was a joy. It was only a narrow structure on a narrow lot, but Mr. Jenkins had compensated by building it seven feet longer than the standard two-bedroom bungalows in that area. The living room allowed us to move freely without bumping into crowded furniture. The dining room, separated from the living room by an archway, was small, but it easily accommodated the sewing machine as well as the dining furniture. We couldn't have wished for any change. In fact, Mr. Jenkins had attended so meticulously to details that each upper corner of the woodwork framing all doorways was unobtrusively decorated with a hand-carved motif.

The windows of both living and dining rooms were fitted with venetian blinds, so there was no need for me to make glass curtains. But as my sewing lessons had included the making of drapes, I willingly took time from my writing to make drapes for the small dining-room window. Those drapes, of ecru linen-like material with a green and brown leaf and twig design, fully lined and with pinch pleats, made me thankful I had taken the sewing course.

Just as Bill and I had admired our first home, the apartment at 1 Homewood Avenue, we now admired our new home, the first we had owned. We gazed with affection at the greens, rusts and gleaming walnut of the furnishings, at our few small oil paintings with touches of blue, and at our big print of Franz Marc's beautifully curved *Red Horses*, which in our print were actually rust. When the sun shone through the south window in the living room, or the west window in the dining room, it cast a glow over the light cream-coloured walls. The general impression was of an invitation to Bill and me, and to any and all visitors, to relax and enjoy the harmony of colour, comfort and contentment.

The rest of the house was equally satisfying. The kitchen was convenient and bright, with white walls and a green and white linoleum-tiled floor. Cupboard knobs and drawer-pulls were red, so I linked the colours by making white curtains with two rows of green ric-rac braid at the hems, and a row of red ric-rac between them. In the name of economy we decided to continue using our little plug-in stove. In any case, however, as we learned later when we could afford a better one, the manufacture of stoves, like that of sewing machines, had been discontinued.

The hot-water heating system was based on a coal-burning furnace, and I thought of Tena tending fires in the north while her husband was away. But I was determined to shovel coal when necessary. Hot water for household use depended on a little iron heater in the basement. It had to be lit with kindling and fed with wood. Anyway, the bungalow was ours, and what did I care what unfamiliar work was involved? What did I care, either, that I had to do the laundry in the basement laundry tubs? I even had an outdoor clothesline, which I appreciated.

The larger of the two bedrooms held our handsome limed-oak furniture with space to spare, and with keen anticipation I took the smaller one for my writing room.

With my own money I paid for my little old portable typewriter to be cleaned, and I bought myself a desk. Bill's tools at that time included only an old hammer and a small saw, but he used them to make me a surprisingly well-balanced bookcase. Then I set the typewriter in place, and was ready to earn my half of our $800 down-payment debt. The room had plenty of space for our davenport, part of our pre-marriage five-dollars-worth of furniture. It would allow me to lie down when necessary, and would allow my mother to use my room as hers when she visited us. I was so happy to settle in at 400 Deloraine Avenue that I couldn't understand why we were the only ones of the Toronto mountie couples to be buying our own home. A few years later I understood perfectly.

At the back of our bungalow we even had a pretty little lawn edged with yellow rose bushes, and space for a little vegetable garden. Bill immediately claimed the garden space, and the following spring he planted the whole patch with his favourite fruit – tomatoes. Our pleasant next-door neighbour had the same size plot, also filled with tomato plants. Each year we lived there the two men vied with each other to produce the bigger crop. Neighbour Bagworth let his plants grow wild. Bill staked his carefully, watered them gently with a spray, and pinched off each shoot that might take valuable nourishment from his carefully chosen fruit-bearing stems.

I believe that if Bill had known then what we heard discussed only later – the value of talking to plants – he would have at least tried that system. In his few spare moments he always went out to see how his tomatoes were developing and, for all I knew, he might have talked to them simply because he cared so much about his "prize" crop. At each harvest time I fervently hoped that Bill's crop would win the contest that was one of his few pleasures. Unfortunately, Mr. Bagworth's untidy tangle of plants, bowed to the ground with bountiful fruit, produced as big a crop as did Bill's scrupulously nurtured, neatly manicured, picture-perfect plants. Each year I was relieved that the men decided they had tied for first place, and so remained friends.

All that came later, of course. Earlier, as soon as we had moved into our bungalow, we had a small disappointment. We noticed that the paint on the walls had faded, leaving darker patches where the Jenkins' pictures had hung. Bill cheerfully planned to repaint the whole interior when he had time, but Mr. Jenkins was very upset.

"I'll provide the paint," he insisted, and so he did.

Soon we became firm friends with him and his wife. As we visited back and forth we were able to provide him with a precious service he hadn't had for decades – a piano accompaniment while he played his violin. On each occasion Bill's singing was a plus, and we could tell that our generous friend felt amply repaid for his kindness to us, although we felt otherwise. Only the Jenkins' dog failed to appreciate the music. Whenever we visited the Jenkins, the dog had to be banished to the basement. There it howled incessantly, although we heard it only faintly.

Meanwhile, Bill and I had settled happily into what had immediately become our cherished home. He was still as busy as ever, often working day and night, and sometimes through the night. Even so, he was eager to do what he could at home. My journal entry for July 1 noted: Holiday. Bill painted bedrooms.

As for me, I was perfectly content to be alone most of the time, steadfastly writing to earn a few dollars in a good cause. Although we were not far from Avenue Road, in those days its traffic noise was only intermittent and not too insistent. I simply put in my ear stopples and went on writing.

Bill found it hard to believe that my hearing was actually as acute as I knew it was. Then one Saturday afternoon as we sat in folding chairs on the deck at the back of our bungalow, he learned that I didn't exaggerate.

I had been so stressed by the noise at 1 Homewood Avenue that I still reacted to any unusual sound, alert to the possibility that it might develop into something that would disturb me. Now, as I sat reading, thankfully aware that there was very little traffic on Avenue road, I suddenly heard a strange sound.

"What's that?" I exclaimed. But Bill couldn't hear anything.

"There it is again!" I said. But he still heard nothing.

"What does it sound like?" he asked.

"I don't know," I said. "I've never heard that kind of sound before."

Bill decided to investigate. I told him the sound came from the direction of the driveway, and he went there to have a look.

"Tell me when you hear it," he called as he looked down the driveway.

"There it is," I called back.

We repeated our back and forth calls several times. Then Bill came back to report. What I'd been hearing was a sparrow intermittently dragging a dried leaf across the concrete driveway at the front of the house, more than fifty feet away from where I sat on the deck. Bill was surprised that I heard such faint sounds. I was less surprised than relieved that I had no need to be concerned that a faint new noise might become loud enough to be a nuisance.

My happiness and peace of mind at 400 Deloraine convinced me that I had at least outgrown my longing for more of the closeness that Bill's work prevented.

A few days after Bill had painted the bedrooms, however, it was my turn to be surprised at what I learned. My mother had come to spend her summer holidays with us, and somehow Bill found time to come with Mom and me to have dinner at the home of friends she and I had known in North Battleford. At that dinner I learned I was wrong about being free of my longing for physical proximity to Bill. The normal seating arrangement placed me between two men I scarcely knew, and Bill elsewhere at the table. I still remember my heartfelt disappointment.

"If only Marion knew how little I see of Bill, and how I ache to be near him," I thought, "she would have ignored protocol and placed me next to my husband."

While Bill worked, Mom and I spent a delightful six weeks together, going to art galleries, museums and movies, visiting friends, and often relaxing in deck chairs on the deck built by the thoughtful Mr. Jenkins overlooking the flower-edged lawn. I wrote each morning, but Mom understood that I must earn money to help repay our Jenkins' debt. Her holiday ended much too soon, and she went back to North Battleford and teaching at King Street school.

I resumed my normal schedule of writing as many hours as I felt equal to it. Bill, of course, still worked as many hours as his workload and his devotion to it demanded. Thus each of us was happy doing what we most enjoyed.

Winter, 1942-43, Toronto. I am wearing my custom-made black Persian lamb coat, and the matching pillbox hat that was a mark-down bargain from Eaton's Annex.

Summer, 1943, Toronto. Our bungalow at 400 Deloraine Avenue. My mother stands at the doorway.

1943, Toronto. Bill with his first crop of tomatoes at 400 Deloraine Avenue.

Bill and I are sunning at the back of our bungalow.

TWENTY

A few weeks after my mother returned to North Battleford, Bill had a surprise telephone call at his office. The caller was Dick Kwan, the thoughtful Chinese waiter who had always had my breakfast set out when I returned by early morning train after visiting Bill at Maidstone. Dick had saved enough money to leave the Dominion Cafe and move to Toronto. He had bought a small restaurant, and wanted us to be his guests at dinner.

The restaurant was very small, with only one row of tables, but the bare wooden tables, like the floor, had been scrubbed scrupulously clean, and the food was excellent. In fact, Dick's older brother, the former cook at the Dominion Cafe, was now working for Dick, as were several of the waiters from that cafe.

Dick told us of his only unhappy experience with the restaurant. He had used every dollar of his savings to buy it, and had no money left to stock it with the absolutely necessary cigarettes. He applied to the Toronto Chinese community organization for a loan, but it was refused. Dick was distraught. Without cigarettes he couldn't open his restaurant. I suppose he was not used to dealing with banks, and didn't think of applying to a bank for a loan. He only knew that his restaurant was ready, but he couldn't open it for business.

A Jew, a stranger who had noticed the work being done, went in to ask how Dick was getting on. Dick, obviously distressed, explained his predicament.

"Get whatever you need," the man said, giving Dick his card. "Tell the wholesaler that I will cover the cost."

Bill and I, like Dick, were amazed that a Jewish stranger had offered to do for a troubled Chinese person what his own people had refused to do.

A week or so later, when Dick came to our home for Sunday afternoon tea, he had another surprise. Naturally I treated him as I would have treated any other guest, but I had to insist that he remain seated while I, in a reversal of roles, waited on him.

Dick's restaurant, which owed its opening to the generosity of a Jewish stranger, was the beginning of his rise to fortune, for which he worked ceaselessly, earning every penny. After four years he sold the restaurant. His total profit to date was $40,000. Bill was duly impressed by the amount, as at that time the RCMP Commissioner, S.T. Wood, earned $10,000 a year. Then Dick bought a pretty little tea room, which he sold after one year. Next he bought a first-class restaurant with white tablecloths, handsome dishes and cutlery, and an attractive, well-stocked bar. The Moon Glow, on north Yonge Street, soon had an affluent and loyal clientele. Even so, I believe that Dick was happiest when Bill and I accepted one of his too-frequent invitations to dinner.

After the Moon Glow came a house, which was soon occupied by Dick's wife and four children from China. Dick calculated the ages of the children from the years he had returned there to visit his wife and family. Eventually Dick Kwan owned the whole block of buildings surrounding his restaurant, plus buildings across the street. But he was still the same soft-spoken gentle Dick we had known at the Dominion Cafe in North Battleford. He hoped that after his death his three sons and one daughter would take over the thriving restaurant.

His children, however, had worked in the Moon Glow after school and during holidays, even while attending university. They had experienced the same fatigue that they knew their father must have endured throughout his working life. So after Dick died, his empire was shared among them, and they prospered in their chosen careers. Bill and I still think fondly of Dick. We consider him a noteworthy example of what could be achieved in those days through ceaseless work and iron determination.

Meanwhile, Bill's working days and nights were as long as Dick's, and although less lucrative, they were at least as productive and satisfying. Rubber had become so scarce that on June 30, 1943 the Wartime Prices and Trade Board had issued Rubber Order No. 4, which further restricted the purchase of new or reconditioned tires and tubes. Hence more and more Canadians broke the law to get the tires and tubes they wanted. And hence Bill and his men spent more and more time tracking them down and preparing for their trials.

One day a constable of the black market squad checked a car with four new tires, and found that the owner was in a nonessential category. The owner-driver explained that he had obtained the tires through Albert Taube, the owner of the Sentry Auto Store. Taube had invited all his customers to apply, through him, for new tires and/or tubes.

Taube's records of permits indicated that seventeen applicants, described as owning panel trucks, which received preference, actually owned passenger cars. Taube had obtained the necessary permits by sending the application forms, either falsified or with some parts left blank, to Eric H. Sanderson, who worked in an office of the Rubber Controller. Just as Glenesk in the Oil Controller's office had accepted bribes and had awarded too-high categories of gasoline ration books, so Sanderson now accepted bribes and allowed tires and tubes for Taube's customers.

Over the next three months, Bill and four of his men investigated. They gathered evidence proving that during July 1943 and the next five months, Taube, Sanderson, and ten others had conspired to commit an offence against Rubber Order No. 4. When the case came to trial in April the following year, all the accused were convicted except the customer who had cooperated with the police.

What amazed me, as I listened to the evidence in court, was the extent of the police work involved. Forty-five witnesses testified, with Bill and his four men heading the list. The mounties produced 156 exhibits, including false applications, tire and tube permits, cancelled cheques, and even the actual tires and tubes, all catalogued for precise identification. The exhibits also included a muskrat fur coat and a slip of paper authorizing the transfer of the coat from one of the conspirators, a wholesale furrier, to a second conspirator. Another slip of paper authorized a further transfer of the coat to conspirator Albert Taube.

The brief of the case, which the police as usual had prepared for the benefit of the crown lawyers who would prosecute, gave all pertinent details of witnesses, exhibits, statements of the accused and so on. It covered seventy-two foolscap-sized pages of double-spaced typing.

No wonder, I thought, that such cases kept Bill busy day and night, weekends and holidays. No wonder, either, that his RCMP work fascinated him to the exclusion of anything else.

There were other time-consuming cases during that same period. One centered on Earl R. Cathcart, an ex-employee of the Oil

Controller's office. He persuaded a woman working at a wicket of one of the offices to steal 1,400 sheets of legitimate gasoline ration coupons. In exchange the foolish woman received rationed goods: thirty pounds of coffee, four pounds of tea, and seven and a half pounds of sugar.

When the case came to trial, sixteen people were proved guilty of being involved in a sale-of-coupons racket. They included, among others: three employees of an aircraft plant; a peddler; a prominent orchestra leader; a man in a paper factory, where his job was to destroy certain coupons for the Oil Controller; and a factory department manager.

While Cathcart was out on bail, one of the black market squad found he had still more coupons in his possession. The police charged him with yet another offence. Bill remarked bitterly that any punishment for that second offence would probably have no effect on Cathcart, since judges still ordered sentences to run concurrently.

By contrast, about the time Bill's men began to investigate Cathcart and the others, a Stockholm dispatch told of three persons put to death in Germany for violations of meat, butter and tobacco rationing laws. Such punishment seemed barbaric, but it indicated how seriously our enemies regarded the effect of black marketeering. An Allied general, in agreement, declared, "To that country which has the last barrel of gasoline will go the victory."

It's a wonder that Bill found time for anything other than work during the three and a half years we lived at 400 Deloraine. But we had occasional visits with the McElhones, the Guernseys and other Mounted Police friends. Unfortunately, one of the couples I liked best had twins at the "terrible-two" stage. On their first visit to us the hyperactive pair tried to climb our living room drapes. So their first visit was also their last.

Bill was always considerate. Whenever possible he arranged his work schedule so that we both could go to events we both enjoyed. We went to some of the summer Promenade concerts, and continued to renew our Eaton's concert series, where we heard excellent performances by such musicians as Marian Anderson, Alexander Kipnis, Helen Jepson, Paul Robeson and Helen Traubel. We also went to see the Volkoff Ballet, one of Canada's first ballet companies, which provided us with our first, thrilling, ballet experience.

When the Chinese Opera Company was stranded in Toronto during the war, our friend Dick Kwan took us to see part of what turned out to be a six-hour performance during which the members of the orchestra ate their lunch. The performance was fascinating. The audience had to imagine a bridge, a river, a storm and so on. At one point an actor shot an arrow from the stage, presumably to some distant place. Twenty minutes later the arrow landed on stage, and the opera continued. In those days there was no television, and I thought that others, especially children, would be interested. So I wrote an article about the Chinese Opera for the *Canadian Red Cross Junior*.

There were other occasions when Bill arranged not to be working, as when we were able to buy ten pounds of sugar as an extra ration. He made sure he was at home the following Sunday, and together we made ten pounds of grape jam and six quarts of peach preserves. My journal also indicates other signs of his thoughtfulness: Bill away. Has arranged for Ted Smith (a member of his squad living nearby) to carry out weekly ashes; Bill away. Left plenty of chopped wood and kindling; Bill away. Brought me a pretty cup and saucer.

Being married to a mountie certainly had disadvantages. But when that mountie was Bill, I found security in believing that he would always show consideration and thoughtfulness. Being a mountie's wife wasn't as bad as it might have been.

TWENTY-ONE

J ust as Bill aimed to please me, so I aimed to please him. My journal noted: Chicken dinner for Bill; made Bill pajamas; bought new-style, dry-and-stretch forms for Bill's socks; and so on. But the same journal pages show that I spent most of my time writing day and night. I mailed Lister article, shadow plays, Chinese Opera article, article to *Shoe and Leather* journal, Grade 2 health workbook and so on. And at last my journal noted: finished paying my half of down payment. After that I paid for gifts to Bill and my mother, for a cleaning woman, and for all my personal expenses, including clothes and dentist's bills.

About the time I finished paying off what I had promised, several ranks of the RCMP had a raise in pay and allowances. Sergeants were slated for an extra one dollar a day, and I immediately planned how best to use it. Unfortunately, the RCMP in those days budgeted at least as strictly as I did. The financial wizards at headquarters noticed that since Regimental No. 12001 became a sergeant, he had been getting an extra one dollar a day as detective pay. Now the RCMP cancelled detective pay for all detectives in the Force, so this resulted in no pay increase for us. Somehow they also juggled living allowances, and we actually had an increase of thirty-five cents a day to add to my budget allowance. Magnanimously the Force allowed Bill to retain his prestigious title of detective. Under the circumstances, however, I didn't feel justified in buying steak instead of sausage, liver or pork shoulder.

In spite of my writing, I made time to sew. My journal noted: made housecoat; midriff nightie; gingham skirt; frilly blouse. And in keeping with the austerity of the time: made sundress from old housecoat. I also helped my neighbour Mrs. Bagworth and others to solve their sewing problems. The needy women included Esther Harrop, whom I had met during our journalism class, and with whom I'd had a warm relationship ever since.

It was easy to find time to help friends during that period as Bill seemed busier than ever, partly because of the scarcity of metal. Its use had been severely restricted since 1942, when the last civilian cars rolled off the assembly lines. At the same time, price ceilings had been placed on all vehicles, including used cars, which couldn't meet increasing demands. Dealers sold them above the ceiling price to the highest bidders, and got rich by doing so. They didn't record the hundreds of dollars above the ceiling price that they collected on each car. In fact, one used-car dealer on Toronto's Danforth Avenue "Automobile Row" made $70,000 in seven months. Obviously Bill and his black market squad had to move in to curb illegal practices.

The scarcity of metal affected me personally. Although we could now afford them, we were unable to buy a washing machine and a bigger and better stove. Moreover, I couldn't even buy pins.

When Esther Harrop asked me to help her make a dress, I cut it out and pinned the pieces together so that she could take them home and baste them. I emphasized that she must return my pins because I couldn't buy any more. When she returned for me to sew the dress, however, she didn't bring them. In spite of my embarrassment, I finally blurted out that I must have my pins back. Esther in turn was greatly aggrieved. Eventually she returned my pins, but our friendship cooled considerably.

At that time, newspapers and magazines carried articles advising women how to cope with shortages of various goods. If Bill had had an old suit to spare, I could have made myself a suit from it. First, the articles said, I should cut down the jacket to make a smaller one. Then I should take the pants apart, turn the pieces upside down, and make a short, slim skirt from the biggest pieces It was important to turn each piece of old material inside out, thus creating the impression of brand new material.

Articles also advised women on how to redo shabby walls and worn linoleum floors. We were to paint the walls and floors, using only one coat of paint instead of the usual two. Then we could hide any thin patches by stippling the whole surface with a second colour of paint, applied very lightly with an uneven sponge.

The painting and stippling sounded like fun. Although our

kitchen floor was still in excellent condition, I decided to redo it in black with white stippling. After the floor was finished, I would update the white curtains by replacing the green ric-rac braid with black, but I'd leave the red ric-rac to tie in with the red knobs and drawer pulls. We were still using our "parish-church-hall" table and chairs, but by now Bill had painted them white. The new effect would be strikingly sophisticated! Black, white and red! And to make sure I had a good foundation, I would use two coats of black paint on the floor.

Unfortunately, the first coat didn't quite dry before my eagerness to finish the job led me to apply the second coat. That made the floor too sticky to walk on.

"It's your problem," Bill told me again and again.

So I set planks on bricks, and we walked on the raised planks for a month. Still the paint didn't dry, and the paint representative failed to help. So I undertook the back-straining job of removing the sticky black paint. Then I had to find someone to help my back return to normal. I found an osteopath, Dr. Hewson, who turned out to be as excellent in his way as my remarkable chiropractor, Dr. Clubine, had been in his. I began having regular treatments again, which made the black-floor episode well worthwhile.

I still had to be careful not to strain my back, and even then I sometimes had serious trouble. One morning I awoke to find that I couldn't get out of bed. With Bill's help I got out and put on my dressing gown. He carried me to the car, and we headed for Dr. Hewson's office in a business building at the corner of Bay and Bloor streets. From where Bill parked the car we moved with the crowd of office workers who stared at the strange sight of a man carrying a woman in a rose-flannel dressing gown. There were more stares as he held me in his arms while we took the elevator to the tenth floor.

Within minutes of Dr. Hewson's treatment I was able to walk. Now other people stared to see the strange couple, a smartly dressed business man and a woman in a rose-flannel dressing gown, walking along the street to a parked car.

By June 1944, about a month after the kitchen was once again white and green, the black market gasoline ration coupons made the most demands on Bill and his men. Counterfeit coupons in particular demanded their attention. There were at least ten different types in circulation in eastern Canada. Toronto was in York county, which had 200,000 registered vehicles, equalling more than twenty-five per cent of all registered vehicles in Ontario. Thus "Toronto the Good" became the most lucrative black market location in Canada for counterfeit coupons.

It was not in Toronto, however, but in Quebec City that Bill had his most notable case of the year. It began when a man in Toronto told Bill that someone in Quebec wanted him to distribute books of counterfeit gasoline ration coupons. Bill asked the informant to send to Quebec for sample books. He expected the man would receive a few, but actually he received 500, which indicated an extensive counterfeit operation.

On July 12 Bill left home for Quebec City where he would work undercover. Before he drove away he assured me he would be back in a day or two. I was used to his being away, but this time it was for seventeen days and nights. During those hectic days, in which members of the Montreal and Quebec City RCMP were also involved, Bill's undercover work brought the investigation to a highly successful conclusion. Not only were the principal offenders discovered and charged, but when Quebec mounties searched the places that Bill indicated, they found counterfeiting equipment, thousands of counterfeit gasoline ration books in various stages of completion, and the press used to print them. Later, Bill received a commendation from Commissioner Wood, a rare gesture.

During the investigation Bill discovered a scandalous political situation in Quebec. The provincial government in power was Liberal, and the opposition party, Duplessis's Union Nationale, hoped to replace it at the coming election. Union Nationale organizers for Quebec City and its environs planned to achieve victory by giving each voter a bottle of moonshine and a book of counterfeit gasoline ration coupons.

Unfortunately for them, Bill's undercover work prevented their dispensing the books of coupons. He never learned what happened regarding the moonshine, but between the end of the investigation and the time of the preliminary hearings, the Union Nationale party formed the government of the province of Quebec.

In mid-October, Bill and those members of the Montreal RCMP who had worked on the case went to Quebec City for the preliminary hearings that would determine whether or not the accused should go to trial. My numerous clippings carried stories by Toronto reporters who also attended the hearings. One wrote that he was amazed at the circus-like proceedings. The Attorney General of the newly-elected government sat on a bench near the two defence counsel, giving advice. From the beginning, those lawyers tried to discredit Bill because he was the crown's most valuable witness.

"Sergeant Kelly is a Mason," one of them told the judge, "so he doesn't believe in God, and so his oath to tell the truth means nothing to him."

The judge disagreed.

At another point, one defence lawyer asked Bill if he was married.

"Yes, I am married," Bill replied.

"How many children do you have?"

"I have no children," Bill answered.

The lawyer threw up his hands and rolled his eyes upward as if this shocking admission, too, disqualified Bill from testifying.

A Toronto *Telegram* reporter wrote that the proceedings were reminiscent of a Gilbert and Sullivan comic opera. When the crown produced its evidence, the defence lawyers pounded on their desks, or flung their arms in all directions and jeered at the police witnesses. At one point a defence lawyer went into hysterics. He screamed at the judge till His Honour had to take temporary refuge in his chambers. One day the Toronto *Telegram* reported that "lawyers became hoarse, the judge became riled, the accused became voluble, and the RCMP was referred to by the defence counsel as a 'gang'."

In spite of all the defence histrionics, the accused were committed for trial. There was no real trial, however. The accused announced that they would plead guilty, so they merely appeared for sentencing. Thus Bill and the other police witnesses had no need to return to Quebec City. The accused appeared before a lenient judge, the choice of whom was influenced by the same Attorney General who had sat near the defence lawyers at the preliminary hearings. In any case, the judge sentenced each guilty person to pay a nominal fine of $1,000.

Bill remarked cynically that in Ontario the guilty persons would have been given long jail terms. In view of the politics involved in this case, however, he believed that they would probably have their fines paid by the Union Nationale party.

My mountie husband sometimes had informants working undercover for him. I met a few of them, but not socially. I didn't meet the most interesting one, however. I only saw him occasionally as I peered through the slats of the almost-closed venetian blinds while he and Bill sat in his car at the front of our house discussing criminal matters.

Pete Mitchell was useful to Bill, and hence to the war effort. On the other hand, he had the reputation of cheating people who were in Canada illegally and who wanted to enter the United States. The police believed that Mitchell promised to take the illegals across the Canadian-American border, a service for which he charged a very high price. Then, it was rumoured, he took them, in the dark of night, to a spot near Niagara Falls. Emphasizing the need for silent caution, he took them over some water to a place he said was in the United States and left them there. In the morning they could see that they were still in Canada, on a peninsula that was part of the Canadian mainland. They didn't get their money back, and presumably they were afraid to complain to the police because they were illegals trying to do something else illegal.

In any case, rumour had it that Pete Mitchell had defrauded a good many would-be illegal emigrants. Rumour also had it, as had rumours about Rocco Perri, that Mitchell sank to the bottom of Lake Ontario, wearing a "cement overcoat".

One morning in mid-December 1944 Bill and I awoke to learn that a twenty-four-inch fall of snow had completely blocked all Toronto streets. Bill put on his high boots and tried to wade through the waist-high Deloraine drifts out to Avenue Road. There he hoped to catch a bus or thumb a ride downtown.

I didn't dare say aloud that I hoped he couldn't get to Avenue Road, but I was secretly glad when he found he couldn't. He came back to the house weary and dejected, explaining that it seemed as if that main thoroughfare was also completely blocked. There was no traffic to be seen or heard. My spirits rose as I knew I had him, housebound, probably for a whole day and night. To my chagrin, I didn't benefit from the situation. Bill spent the whole day and part of the night telephoning and making notes, or moping because he couldn't get to work. In those days I'd never heard the word "workaholic", but I certainly was well acquainted with the concept.

Early next morning the snowplows finished clearing the Toronto streets, and Bill went back to his beloved work. Many hours before that, however, I realized that I was still firmly entrenched in square one.

TWENTY-TWO

When World War II ended in Europe in August 1945, I presumed that consumer goods would soon be available, that restrictions would soon be lifted, and that Bill would soon be less busy. I was wrong on all three points, especially the third. Scarcities and restrictions continued, and so did Bill's heavy work schedule.

Just as I had accepted the fact that I couldn't spend much time with Bill during the war, I now accepted it because, even after the war, his work was still of vital importance. I was less acquiescent that fall when the RCMP initiated the program Youth and the Police, and Bill was detailed for the extra work of taking charge of the program in Toronto and district. I heaped silent scorn on the Force that in my opinion so ruthlessly overworked my husband. Now he would be busier than ever, with much of the new work done in the evening, while some mounties had regular office hours, daytime only.

Nevertheless, I recognized the value of the Youth and the Police movement. I learned that originally a Mounted Policeman in a Manitoba town of mixed nationalities had organized recreational facilities for young people, and had made friends with them. Juvenile delinquency fell by eighty per cent. Commissioner Wood planned that, after the war, other mounties would present themselves to young people as friends. So Bill and his men, like other mounties across Canada, visited schools, church groups, boys' clubs and industrial schools. They gave talks, showed films and answered questions. They found that the young people were interested in everything, from police service dogs like Dale of Cawsalta to work in the far north. By the end of the series they were even interested in Discipline and Courtesy.

Bill was so impressed that he wrote an article on Youth and the Police. It was published in the *RCMP Quarterly* magazine, and also in the Commissioner's Annual Report of that year. At Bill's request I was his home-based editor and rewrite woman which, as he said then and often repeated later, gave him confidence in anything he sent out. I was glad to help. Besides, how could he later complain when I got a couple of articles on the subject for myself?

About the same time Bill and his men began working on Youth and the Police, they had extra work from meat rationing, which was imposed in mid-September. Many Canadians were not satisfied with the ration allowance of about ten pounds a year, which was more than the Canadian average yearly consumption before the war. Apparently they paid no attention to newspaper reports of people in some European cities queuing up for their only meal of the day, a handout of boiled sugar beets. In any case, many heartless Canadians violated meat regulations and ceiling prices.

After the Thomas Meat Market on north Yonge Street was fined three times for selling above the ceiling price, the store's licence was cancelled. The owner's wife showed no sign of remorse. She merely retorted sharply that closing the store was a foolish thing for the government to do.

"They'll be losing $7,000 in income tax," she snapped.

My writing over that last year had gone extremely well, although I simply accepted the situation as normal. Looking back over the years, however, I can see that other people must have appreciated my writing more than I did. I had submitted articles and verses to Sunday School papers in Canada and the United States, and articles to trade journals and a country magazine in Canada, and everything had been accepted.

Miss Howatt was always pleased with what I wrote for School Publications. When I told her that I wanted to be paid four dollars a page, instead of the three dollars which was standard for all of her writers, she agreed at once.

"We must keep you happy," she smiled.

That same year Copp Clark planned to publish a new set of school readers for Grades 4, 5 and 6. They would be in line with their splendid Grades 1, 2 and 3 readers on which I had based my songbook *Highroads to Singing*. Editor Claude Lewis scanned back issues of the *Canadian Red Cross Junior* magazine, looking for pieces to reprint and for the names of possible writers for his project. As a result, he used three of my articles from the magazine and three commissioned pieces. One of the latter was the rewrite of an incoherent story about Australia that another writer had done for him.

At Mr. Lewis's request I copy-edited several other articles. Then he offered me a job as copy editor at one dollar an hour. That was much more than I earned as a writer, but I preferred writing. I declined the opportunity to become a copy editor.

Miss Browne was always satisfied with my work, and sometimes telephoned to tell me so as soon as she had read what I sent her. She asked me to be her assistant editor, part time, at $100 a month. The understanding was that I would become the editor in about a year, when she would retire.

It was a tempting offer, not only because of the money, but also because I admired Miss Browne very much. I knew I would have enjoyed working with her. Also, I would have enjoyed the opportunity to influence the magazine's young readers. But at the time Miss Browne made the offer, Bill was hearing rumours of Mounted Police transfers to take place soon after the war ended. I felt that in fairness to her I must decline her tempting offer, and I shed a few tears as I did so.

The year 1946 began as 1945 had ended. Bill worked and I wrote, and both of us enjoyed what we were doing.

I also enjoyed our comfortable and attractive bungalow. ("As pretty as a doll's house," one elderly visitor had remarked.) I would have been perfectly happy to have lived there, writing, for the rest of my life. And of course I still had my special friends. They not only shared my main interest, but they also pleased both my mother and me by making a fuss over her during her summer holiday visit each year.

Early in 1946 Bill went to Ottawa for several weeks. There he helped sift the mass of evidence gathered by the RCMP after Igor Gouzenko, a cipher clerk at the Soviet Embassy in Ottawa, had defected to Canada. Gouzenko had exposed a widespread Communist espionage system that threatened the safety of Canada. Some Canadians scoffed that we had no secrets worth stealing. They refused to consider that Canadian files also contained the vitally important secrets of the U.S.A. and Great Britain, and that these, too, were the targets of the spies in Canada.

Incidentally, Gouzenko later sometimes confided in the mounties who protected him. On one occasion he admitted that his defection was at least partly triggered by the abundance of consumer goods in Canada, available for anyone to buy. He and his wife could hardly believe that they could purchase anything they saw in the big grocery chain stores in Ottawa, even bacon and fresh fruit.

Almost as soon as Bill returned from Ottawa, he and his men learned that a tailor named Morgenstern was selling men's suits above the ceiling price. The tailor explained to a plainclothes mountie that he had to charge more than the ceiling price for his suits. His problem was that the wholesale textile company he dealt with demanded more than the ceiling price for the cloth from which he made his suits. Thus began one of the most notable textile investigations of the whole wartime and post-war period. The police traced the above-the-ceiling offences to the Shiffer Lightman Company, owned by Joseph Jack Shiffer and his father, Abraham Shiffer. If tailors and retailers refused to pay extra, the Shiffers would refuse to sell to them, thus driving them out of business.

When I attended the trials, I learned that the wholesalers had extracted about $60,000 in bonuses from their customers. The Shiffers pleaded guilty and paid fines on forty-eight charges of selling goods above the ceiling price, and of issuing false invoices. Jack Shiffer was also sentenced to nine months in jail, but his father escaped a prison sentence because of his heart condition.

Later the Shiffers were also convicted and fined in connection with false income tax returns. The tailors and retailers involved were also charged under the price ceiling regulations, and they in turn were fined. Later they, too, had to pay penalties for income tax infractions.

After the trials I worked out all the Shiffers' profits and fines, and I saw that they were still financially ahead. Such was the attitude of certain judges regarding violations of Canadian laws. Perhaps they didn't bother to add and subtract as I did. In any case I, like Bill, was growing more and more cynical.

As the year 1946 progressed, some wartime regulations were removed, and Bill's work eased somewhat. Also, manufacturers began making such peacetime products as stoves and washing machines. Although the output didn't meet the demands, in early August we were lucky enough to buy one of each.

Of course I was delighted to have a washing machine, but I was overwhelmed with joy at having the stove. It was the biggest Moffatt, with a big oven with top and bottom elements, and with four elements on the top of the stove, all of which I could use at the same time. Constantly I wiped the stove's gleaming white surface with a soft cloth, sometimes pausing to stroke it as gently as I would have stroked a pet kitten.

That stove meant much more to me than a convenient means of

cooking. It meant the beginning of the end of wartime regulations, with less work for Bill, and more time for us to be together. Thanksgiving that year was the best one yet, not simply because of the delicious meal produced on our marvellous new stove, but because of the happier future it symbolized.

Mid-November of that year was even more exhilarating. I had written a series of articles on such world leaders as Mackenzie King, Churchill, Roosevelt, Stalin and Chiang Kai Shek for the *Canadian Red Cross Junior*, and I had asked Mr. C.J. Eustace, editor of Dent and Sons, Canada, if he would like to publish a book of those articles. Yes, he would like to, but only if I would be the editor for a series of such books. I didn't want to be an editor of other people's books, so I declined.

Then, because my research while writing articles on the RCMP had given me a broad general knowledge of that organization, I suggested to Mr. Eustace that I should write a history of the Force. During my research I had noticed that most of the accurate histories were rather dry, with extra-long paragraphs and a lot of tiresome statistics. On the other hand, the interesting ones contained a lot of fiction, and only an expert could tell which was which. I proposed writing a history that was absolutely factual, but also highly readable. Mr. Eustace agreed.

With great enthusiasm I immediately set to work. During the next four weeks I bought all available writings about the Force, and I spent countless hours at general and reference libraries. Then I knew I could write the kind of history I aimed at. It was exciting! I, a woman, was going to venture into the realm of the male-only organization that too often ignored even the existence of its camp followers. Moreover, I would produce such a good book that even the Mounted Police would have to recognize me as an individual.

In mid-December I suddenly became less confident. On December 17, Bill learned that he had been promoted to the rank of sub/inspector, and we knew that after two years of satisfactory service and his passing certain examinations, he would become a full inspector. He was to be transferred to Ottawa as soon as was convenient. There he would be a personnel officer for several divisions.

There was no time that evening for us to discuss the promotion or the move. Bill was busy as usual, this time at the prestigious Granite Club, giving a talk on Youth and the Police. But I, also as usual, was delighted for Bill's sake about the promotion. And the next day I felt the familiar surge of admiration as I added yet another clipping, with a photo, to my scrapbook.

"One of the youngest officers in the RCMP to attain the rank of inspector," the Toronto *Telegram* reported, "is W.H. Kelly, 35."

That young officer assured me that my life as an officer's wife would be infinitely more pleasant than it had been as the wife of a lowly constable or a middle-status NCO. There would be more money to spend, and when an officer was transferred, the Force even paid for the movers to do the packing, whereas the lower ranks had to do their own.

"And of course we'll be socializing with officer-class people in the future," Bill assured me. Already Assistant Commissioner Marsom, OC of "O" Division, had been in touch with Bill. He had said that Mrs. Marsom would call me and invite us to tea.

As for Bill's new work, he admitted that he'd have to travel a lot. But he could arrange his own work schedule, he announced, so he would spend more time at home.

"Everything will be different now, different and better," he told me again and again.

My problem was that I didn't want everything to be different. I wanted to stay in the same convenient bungalow in the same reference-rich city, writing the same history book that I hoped would establish me as an individual in the same organization that was about to tear me up by the roots.

Instead, the only constant in our new situation was that Bill would be away from home a great deal. Furthermore, we'd have the disruption of moving, and the difficulty of finding an apartment in over-crowded, post-war Ottawa.

As for the stove, my gleaming symbol of happier times to come, Bill insisted we couldn't use it in an apartment that would undoubtedly have its own stove. Reluctantly I accepted reality once more. After owning my wonderful stove for only two months, I sold it to my grateful neighbour, Mrs. Bagworth. At the same time I relinquished my ill-founded dreams of a companionable home life.

One thing I was determined not to relinquish, though – writing my RCMP history book and so earning recognition as a worthy individual. Otherwise, now that Bill's unusually early promotion to sub/inspector proved his superiority, I was even more likely to have no identity other than as his wife. Although we would now be associating with "officer-class" people, I couldn't be sure how the officers would regard me. Perhaps they would be no more polite and sociable than the lower ranks had been at their Christmas parties.

In those earlier days, my situation as the wife of a constable or an NCO had been somewhat similar to my situation during the time of Maestro M. and his singing students' recitals. At that time Bill was the acknowledged star and I was merely his wife, although my musical knowledge and ability had helped him achieve that stardom, which Maestro M. knew but ignored.

I didn't realize the similarity of the situations until about fifty years later, as I was checking everything before completing this book. However, in mid-December 1946 I did realize, beyond the slightest doubt, that I must write my book.

1946, Toronto. Bill the day he was promoted to sub-inspector. Photo taken at the insistence of other officers. He is wearing a cap and jacket borrowed from another officer.

TWENTY-THREE

S oon after Bill was promoted to sub/inspector, he was offered a position outside the Force by Norman L. Mathews,
Q.C. Mr. Mathews headed the well-known Toronto law
firm of Mathews, Stivers and Lyon. He knew Bill since he had often
been the crown prosecutor for Bill's black-market cases.

Bill, as usual, had amassed and arranged the evidence for those
cases with meticulous care, and Mr. Mathews greatly admired his
ability. Now he offered Bill a position in his law firm, although Bill
had no law degree and not even a university education. Mr. Mathews
offered to fund Bill's attendance at university while he obtained a law
degree. During that time Bill would work in the law office as his time
permitted, specializing in labour relations, and acting as an arbitra-
tor in labour disputes.

At that point in his career Bill had no intention of leaving the
Force, so he declined the offer. I quite understood that Bill didn't
want to be a lawyer any more than I wanted to be an editor. But I
thought wistfully that if he had accepted Mr. Mathews' offer we
would have stayed in Toronto. I didn't try to persuade him to change
his mind.

For the first few days after Bill's promotion to sub/inspector, I
felt both rich and privileged. Not only did I expect to have lot more
money to handle, but my new women friends would be officers'
wives who would, I presumed, be as superior in their own way as Bill
had led me to believe their husbands were in theirs. I hoped they

wouldn't be too far above me.

My high-flying expectations soon gave way to reality. Bill was indeed getting more money now, even more than our milk delivery man. But whereas in the past he'd been provided with either his uniform or a clothes allowance, as an officer he had to buy all uniforms. This was so even though he would still be working in plain clothes, but without any plain-clothes allowance.

He needed a working outfit of brown serge tunic, blue breeches, high boots and spurs; a dressier outfit of navy blue tunic, blue overalls (close-fitting tapered trousers with foot straps) and half-Wellington, ankle-high boots; a red serge tunic to wear on certain occasions with the breeches and high boots; and a mess kit of short red serge jacket and a dark blue waistcoat to be worn with the blue overalls at such functions as regimental dinners, New Year's levees, and dances. He also needed a heavy, medium-length, blue peajacket for cold weather wear with most uniforms and, for ceremonial occasions, a swashbuckling heavy blue broadcloth cape with a glorious scarlet lining.

In addition there were such extras as a stetson, a fur cap, a peaked cap trimmed with gold braid, a brown leather Sam Browne military-style belt with over-the-shoulder strap, and a gold-embroidered belt for dress wear. And of course he needed an expensive sword, with a brown leather scabbard for use with the Sam Browne, and a silver-coloured metal scabbard for use with the gold belt. In addition to all this he must now buy all his uniform-style shirts, socks and ties, since the annual issue of such items was provided only for constables and NCOs.

In those days the Force gave its new officers a one-time clothing grant of $200. But the necessary pair of excellent-quality high boots cost $60 (the equivalent in the late 1990s of about $750). Obviously the remaining $140 wouldn't go far. So I stopped feeling rich. Then I budgeted for Bill's repayment, by way of monthly cheque deductions, for everything he must buy through the RCMP.

My research into RCMP history has shown me that officers' purchase of their own uniforms and equipment was one of the things that set them apart from the lower ranks. The custom went back to 1873, when the original officers of the North-West Mounted Police had to provide their own uniforms. They were even expected to purchase their own saddles, as most of them eventually did. Indeed, some wealthy officers even purchased their own horses. I presume that the custom was a carry-over from the age-old British army tradition by which only persons of wealth and privilege were considered fit to be leaders. And of course they could easily provide for themselves.

In any case, the original officers of the NWMP were so far removed from the lower ranks that, although by 1873 Canada had been united in Confederation for six years, they received their commissions not from the Canadian government but from Queen Victoria. Therefore they didn't sign on with other members of the Force. Nor did they have regimental numbers, although in the mid-1890s officers were numbered separately, and the earlier ones were back-numbered.

Bill became 0. 375, but he was not required to use his number. Formerly he'd had to sign himself officially as "W.H.Kelly, Regimental No. 12001", but now he signed as "W.H.Kelly, sub/inspector". It gave the impression that when a man was promoted to the rank of officer he was no longer a mere number, but an individual, a member of a select group. Even his salary was no longer calculated as daily pay and allowances but as an annual salary, $2,456.25 for sub/inspector.

The segregation was undoubtedly necessary for discipline, and in general a higher rank usually indicated more ability. But even at the time Bill was promoted, there also seemed to be an indefinite something else that put officers on pedestals, probably relating to the original perception of officers as members of the privileged wealthy class. Certainly the Force's officers have always been a noticeable minority, as is natural in any such organization. According to Bill's new number, there had been only 375 officers in the almost three-quarters of a century of the Force's history. At the time of his promotion, 100 of them were currently serving members, while the lower ranks at that time numbered about 2,500.

In spite of the officers' mystique, however, from my point of view Bill the officer was the same person as Bill the NCO or even Bill the constable. This affected my judgement of the other officers. I now changed my opinion of the officer who had asked (or was it ordered?) Constable Bill to sing at his wedding. He knew that Bill and I were married, but I was not invited to the ceremony. Bill had not seen anything wrong with that, and I accepted my exclusion as a lower-ranking wife. A year or so later, when Corporal Bill pointed out that same officer in a supermarket, I was still so indoctrinated that I didn't consciously resent the wedding incident. I simply felt astonished that so exalted a person was pushing a cart of groceries just as we lesser mortals were doing. But now that Bill was an officer, and I was one of "them", I perceived things differently. I was like the child who saw that the emperor's new clothes didn't exist. Privately I characterized the offending officer as boorish.

To my later regret, soon after Bill had been promoted and had left for Ottawa, I myself was boorish in my lack of courtesy to two officers' wives. I met them at the OC's Sunday afternoon welcoming tea, where all was dignity and decorum. Soon they invited me for tea with just the two of them. I accepted gladly, anticipating my first friendship with officers' wives.

Impatiently I waited for the day of the tea, which indicated that my hostesses were offering me new and approved friendship. I presumed that my new friends would be something like the only other officer's wife I had known previously – Mrs. Frank Spriggs, the wife of Bill's OC at North Battleford. She was a cultured and gracious woman whom I had admired during our common involvement with various musical groups. Now I was happy to be making exalted friends, and happy to be pleasing Bill by becoming integrated into the officers-and-wives social set.

The moment we three began our tea, I saw I had moved into a higher class. There were assorted dainty sandwiches and expensive French pastries, both obviously bought specially for the occasion, and rich cream for the tea. My strict budget had always forced me to classify such things as forbidden luxuries, so that we could afford other such luxuries as season concert tickets at Eaton Auditorium, and at the same time buy our share of war savings certificates.

The conversation was less exalted than I had expected. My new friends didn't read books, or go to lectures, plays or concerts. They didn't even listen to outstanding radio programs, and in those days there was no television to discuss. I was soon out of my element. The three-way conversation became a two-way chattering of scandalous gossip, mostly relating to peculiar sex habits, pregnancies, miscarriages, and the questionable activities of other officers' wives.

If I had expected less, I'd have been less shocked. It wasn't even the things those women talked about that disturbed me as much as that they seemed to have nothing else to talk about. Soon I was to learn that my two strange hostesses were rare exceptions among the wives of Bill's new confreres, just as I was to learn that the offensive officer was also a rare exception. At the time of that afternoon tea, however, I was so disenchanted that I didn't invite my hostesses in return. That of course was unforgivable, and probably marked the beginning of my reputation for being anti-social.

Actually, I wasn't really anti-social in the months after Bill's promotion. A truer classification would have been "un-social". I wasn't against socializing; I simply hadn't any time or energy for it. I was trying desperately to do as much work as possible on my book before the impending upheaval of moving. At the same time I was busier than usual with household affairs.

Bill had gone to Ottawa early in January 1947, leaving me in Toronto until he could find a place for us to live in that over-crowded, post-war capital city. Actually, the police-rented house there was reserved for the officer holding the position that Bill now had. Normally we'd have had the use of it, paying the rent by way of a deduction from Bill's monthly cheque. But my *bête noire* officer had also been transferred to Ottawa, and he used his seniority to claim "our" house for himself.

So Bill, along with two other recently transferred officers, scouted the city for any available housing. At last they found a small apartment house under construction. With typical Mounted Police perseverance they tracked down the owner and persuaded him to rent apartments to them the moment the building was completed.

Meanwhile, I had spent countless hours at Toronto libraries and bookstores, and at my desk and typewriter. Numerous other things also demanded my attention. As long as winter lingered I had to tend the coal furnace constantly, although I still had help taking out the ashes. Also, as we hadn't felt we could afford to change the wood-burning basement heater for an electric one, I had to provide kindling and wood. To solve the food problem, because of no convenient bus service, I used a bundle buggy to haul groceries four very long blocks. In that way I also managed the regular twenty-pound food parcels for Bill's parents.

When the contract for my book finally came from Dent, I attended to the details myself. I also went to Hamilton to see Miss Howatt of School Publications. My back gave out from time to time, so I had to make more trips to my osteopath. Bill came home two or three times to attend court for the cases still pending from his NCO days, and he always did everything he could to help, but his visits were inevitably cut short because of his urgent work in and out of Ottawa.

On one occasion he came home to attend the Supreme Court in Toronto. He was needed to give evidence in a case against the Wool Administrator. That official still operated his own wholesale wool import company. He was charged under the wartime wool regulations with rearranging the established priority system so that his company unfairly obtained more than its rightful share of woollen cloth. Evidence proved that he had made a profit of $40,000 on the wool he had received illegally. The accused was found guilty and sentenced to a term in the penitentiary.

Selling our bungalow while Bill was in Ottawa posed another problem for me. Two real estate agents in succession listed it for thirty days each, and my writing had been constantly interrupted.

Dozens of potential buyers came to inspect the bungalow, always dawdling to praise its splendid construction. But the agents, against our advice, had overpriced it at $9,600, and didn't sell it.

In mid-April, Bill announced that the Ottawa apartment would be ready by the end of the month. I set about selling the bungalow myself, with the price set at a realistic $8,000. I placed seductive advertisements in the weekend Toronto newspapers. That same weekend I had almost sixty responses by telephone, and I conducted about fifteen tours of inspection. That brought me one potential buyer, who asked for a $300 reduction if he paid in cash. He probably expected me to bargain. But I decided that forty per cent profit on our original purchase was quite enough, and I jumped at his offer.

Then I dashed about, seeing to everything before leaving Toronto. To the lawyers to finalize the sale of the bungalow in the approved manner. To the hairdresser for a permanent so that I wouldn't have to bother with one once I got down to writing in Ottawa. To the dentist because I'd learned it was difficult to find an available dentist in post-war Ottawa. To visit Miss Browne at Red Cross headquarters, to visit friends to say goodbye, to the reference library in case I might find something I'd missed earlier. To my osteopath because I didn't know how long it would be before I found a good one in Ottawa. And to my general practitioner to discover why I was so tired and how I could get more energy for finishing my book.

The moving of an officer's household goods was accomplished just as Bill had said it would be. When the movers came, on Monday, May 5, they were prepared to do all the packing. Even so, I made sure that each box was correctly labelled as to contents, and I packed my own notes, research books and typed material. I cleaned out the refrigerator, supervised the transfer of the gleaming white stove of my dreams to my friendly next-door neighbour, Mrs. Bagworth. I closed hydro and telephone accounts, and made sure that all cupboards, clothes closets and floors were left as scrupulously clean as the Jenkins had left them for us.

By evening the movers had gone, and I had finished the cleaning. Sitting on a garden chair I was leaving behind, I waited for one of Bill's former black market squad me to drive me to the station, where I would take the night train to Ottawa.

By the time he came I was still so exhausted that, as soon as I got into the front seat of the police car with him, I slumped forward and rested my head on my folded arms against the dashboard. We were halfway to the station before I could sit upright, and even then I could scarcely talk. But I wouldn't have felt like engaging in pleasant conversation anyway. My driver happened to be the man who had told Bill not to mind that I was so anxious and unhappy during the second year of our married life. For all I knew, Constable G. still thought that I was unworthy of being the wife of a Mounted Policeman and that "even Jesus Christ couldn't please Nora".

As soon as I boarded the train and found the compartment Bill had reserved for me, I undressed, crawled into the already made-up bed, and fell into a deep sleep. I awoke to find the porter rousing me. It was morning, and the train would soon arrive in Ottawa.

TWENTY-FOUR

It was wonderful to be reunited with Bill. I was less pleased about the apartment on McKay Street, although Bill had done his best. We had one of the top two of four very small apartments above ground. Two other RCMP officers had the apartments on the first floor, and a civilian had the apartment beside ours. The owner and his family had a bigger one in the basement. Probably because of post-war scarcities, the building was of flimsy construction. Sounds carried alarmingly. In the daytime I could hear the frequent crying of the baby immediately below. In the night we could hear the loud snoring from an apartment even farther away. But there was no danger of our music disturbing the other tenants. Neither the stairs nor any window had allowed the movers to bring in our piano, so it had gone into storage. The outdoor noises were worse than those indoors. Streetcars rattled past the corner only a couple of hundred feet away. Children in the schoolyard backing on the apartment house shrieked and screamed at recess, noon, and before and after school. Worst of all was the firehall across the street. When there was no need for the firemen to drive their clanging trucks to a fire, they dashed in and out of the firehall on reverberating practice runs up and down and around McKay Street. I remembered reading about a noted writer who often complained to his wife about the cat stomping outside his closed door. I wondered what he would have said about our noises.

Concentration was impossible. Even my ear stopples, pushed in painfully tight, couldn't give me the quiet I needed. By this time I had made notes on all the available books about the NWMP, the RNWMP, and the RCMP, and I was well along with the approximately sixty issues of the *RCMP Quarterly* magazines. My next task would be to study the seventy-three annual reports, published since 1874, which contained important information about the development of the Force. The only way I could work with confidence was to keep all details in mind for easy coordination. But I simply couldn't remember everything while I was bombarded with noise.

I felt hopeless. I blamed the Force that had transferred Bill, and the officer who had robbed us of the house that would have let me write in peace. I ached with longing to give up my project, but I wouldn't admit defeat. Anyway, even if I gave it up, I still couldn't have any settled home life with Bill, who always had to put his work ahead of everything else.

Bill was sympathetic, but after my first week at McKay Street he was away much of the time. His new job as Divisional Personnel Officer was quite demanding, since it covered Divisions of "O" (western Ontario), "A" (eastern Ontario), "N" (Training, Rockcliffe), and "G" (the Yukon and the Northwest Territories).

The Personnel Department had been established only recently, in 1944, for the benefit of individual constables and NCOs, and for the efficiency of the whole organization. DPOs interviewed, assessed and reported on applicants for engagement, recruits in training and serving members. They also gave them an opportunity to discuss their personal and service problems. Creation of the new department was a great step for the organization that seemed formerly to have been directed with little or no concern for the lower ranks. Getting it into operation, however, entailed a tremendous amount of work. Bill was constantly on the road, opening new applicant files and doing follow-up interviews in Divisions "O", "A" and "N". The work in the "G" Division was held over for the future.

Fortunately, he was at home enough to see how frustrated I was at not being able to concentrate. He located a constable who lived a few blocks along McKay Street who was willing to let me rent his attic. The constable's house was within walking distance, in a very quiet spot opposite the Governor-General's grounds. Its attic bedroom furniture included a big table and a wooden chair. Fortunately for me, the constable's family was away for the summer, so I'd be alone in the house. Before the middle of June I moved in, with all my paraphenalia and with great hopes.

Unfortunately, that June in Ottawa was one of the hottest on record for many years. The outdoor temperature often reached

94 degrees Farenheit, and the temperature in my attic seemed higher. There was probably not much insulation in the ceiling, and as the constable's family didn't use the attic, the storm windows had been left on.

I could scarcely breathe. I removed most of my clothes, set a basin of water beside me on the table, and with my left hand I constantly dabbed myself with a dripping washcloth while I wrote with my right. Before long the heat and the frequent thunderstorms got the better of me. I worked opposite the Governor-General's pastoral grounds for one month only.

Back at home, the heat was almost as oppressive, and the noise continued to be overwhelming. For the rest of the summer I gained a little relief at night by opening the back door that led from our cramped kitchen to a tiny balcony, and I slept on the chesterfield cushions laid out on the kitchen floor. Then, although I am normally a night person, I got up at 4:30 a.m., and worked in peace for at least a few hours each day.

As the summer progressed I thought only of writing, and Bill and I quarrelled as we had done a few years earlier. I couldn't blame him for believing we never should have married. Our living-dining room looked like a junk shop of used books and papers, which I refused to tidy away because I needed everything at hand. Obviously we couldn't invite anyone to visit us. And because I didn't want to tire my already tired back still more, I complained even about having to go downstairs to play cribbage with friends. They were Inspector Tony McKinnon, whom Bill admired, and his wife, Dora, a paragon of wifely and culinary virtues. I, by contrast, lacked such desirable qualities. I admitted to myself that I deserved Bill's reproof.

Even doing the laundry was a problem. The cramped little kitchen had no space for the washing machine, so it had been forced out on the tiny back balcony. I lacked the strength and stability to drag it into the kitchen near the sink, so I had to wash on a day when Bill was home to drag it in for me. Often Sunday was his only day at home, and then the other officers' wives would see me hanging the washing on the balcony clothesline.

"You dirty protestant!" Dora shouted up at me one Sunday morning.

I realized later that she had only been joking, but at the time I felt hurt. I gave up Sunday washing, but didn't explain the situation. Fortunately, soon after that a do-it-yourself, coin-operated laundry, one of the first in Ottawa, opened only a few blocks away. So Bill and I carried our bundles back and forth at his convenience.

In spite of all problems, the more battered by circumstances I felt, the more determined I was to finish my history of the Force. By this time I had an additional reason to keep on writing: I had come to admire the early Mounted Policemen who, in the face of terrible odds, had achieved great things. Although I disliked and resented the organization that so adversely affected me, I wanted to tell its story.

I still admired Bill, too. But at the same time I became so distraught that I believed I'd never have any peace until I died, or until he died and left me free of him and his demanding work. But one Sunday evening in mid-August I learned that I didn't really want to be free.

He had left that afternoon by train to be in Toronto early Monday morning. A few hours later he telephoned to say that he was safe, although he had been in a train wreck. As his train had rounded a curve its brakes had failed, and the locomotive and the first few cars had toppled over. The brakeman had been killed, and others severely injured. Bill was in the dining car at the back of the train. He was shaken but safe.

"Safe, safe, safe!" I kept saying aloud after I'd hung up. Then suddenly I visualized the alternative, and I began to tremble. Shaking, I made my way downstairs to our cribbage friends, and they calmed me till at last I was able to walk back upstairs and stay alone.

No! No! No! I didn't want to be free of Bill! Still trembling, I undressed and fell into bed, but as soon as I closed my eyes I saw Bill lying beside the wreck, dead . . .

In the autumn I tried to please him by going to teas given by various officers' wives, although we both knew that attendance was something of a command performance. Perhaps that was because Commissioner Wood looked back to the early 1900s and life with father, Assistant Commissioner Zachary Taylor Wood. The assistant commissioner was the grandson of Zachary Taylor, the twelfth president of the United States, and considered protocol important. In any case, Commissioner Wood considered it important for the officers' wives, like the officers themselves, to carry on the tradition of forming cohesive social groups.

Fortunately, at the first tea of the season, given by Mrs. Wood, I found that even the commissioner's wife was friendly and approachable. As for the other women, they, too, shone by contrast with my two strange hostesses in Toronto. Even so, the hierarchy of wives, linked to the hierarchy of officers, was always respected.

The more I socialized, the more I fretted about wasting time. I willingly regularly left my writing to help our friendly landlord's children speak fluent English, because they were at a great disadvantage with French only. But I begrudged time spent at afternoon teas or at social evenings devoted solely to discussions of Mounted Police affairs. Understandably, the more I avoided socializing, the more I was considered anti-social by other Mounted Police people. Bill was still reluctant to let them know that I was intruding on his territory by writing about his organization, so scarcely anyone knew what I was doing. Thus I was judged according to how I did or did not participate in what all officers' wives were expected to do in those days.

My feeling of frustration and inadequacy led to such exhaustion, physical and mental, that I could no longer judge if my writing was up to my normal standard. Mr. Eustace and Miss Blackstock, my personal editor at Dent, had approved the first third of my book, but as time went on I could only follow my original plan and hope for the best.

Bill helped me by not coming home for lunch when his work kept him in Ottawa. One noontime someone telephoned for him, identifying himself as Deputy Commissioner Gagnon. All morning I'd been harrassed by noises, and that telephone interruption was the last straw. I forgot the respect due to a highly placed officer.

"Sorry," I said, my voice noticeably cool. "Bill stays downtown for lunch these days."

"Stays downtown for lunch!" The deputy commissioner gasped as if he could scarcely believe such an astonishing behaviour by one of his officers.

I was immediately on the defensive for having failed to accede to the rights and privileges of an RCMP officer at lunchtime.

"Yes!" I responded sharply. "He's staying downtown so he won't interrupt me in the middle of the day. Don't you ever give your wife a break in the middle of the day?"

"Perhaps, sometimes," Deputy Commissioner H.A.R. Gagnon admitted, and closed the conversation.

I was immediately so ashamed of my thoughtless impertinence that I didn't tell Bill about it, and I dreaded having to meet the deputy commissioner sometime. Realizing that my fanatical devotion to my book was becoming dangerous, I took three weeks off and wrote a second health workbook for School Publications. I had just got back to my history book when an Ottawa newspaper reported that the deputy commissioner would become commissioner early the following year, when Commissioner Wood was due to retire. Then I became obsessed with the fear that his even more lofty disapproval as commissioner might fall on Bill as well as on me.

As it happened, my fears were unfounded. Deputy Commissioner Gagnon died suddenly in November 1947, and took my secret to the grave. If I ever turn to writing fiction I'll be able to depict, with absolute realism, the relief of a criminal at the death of the only witness against him.

The festive Christmas season led to the officers' New Year's Eve dance. For that notable occasion I'd had to stop writing to make a black crepe evening dress. It was sleeveless with epaulet shoulders and an almost circular skirt that undulated gracefully with every movement. The effect was enhanced with silver jewellery. The other women looked as if they, too, had done their best, but the men far outshone us. After nonchalantly flinging off their scarlet-lined capes, the resplendent officers danced in scarlet mess jackets, blue overalls, half-Wellingtons and spurs, and white gloves. The scarlet tunics of the RCMP orchestra and the multicoloured lights revolving in the ceiling completed a scene glamorous enough to satisfy even a Hollywood director.

An infrequent glamorous occasion, however, was not enough to keep us happy in Ottawa. Besides, although the snow had dampened some outdoor noises, one noise now stood out above the others. The school immediately behind us had a fenced-in outdoor skating rink, and during out-of-school hours the noise reached a painful decibel level. Day and night I heard the constant thud-thud of would-be hockey stars slamming one another against the boards. Often other children contributed more noise as they shouted encouragement or shrieked their disapproval.

By this time post-war scarcities had eased off, and construction of all kinds was well under way. Bill and I decided to buy a house.

At noon on Tuesday, February 3, 1948, we chose a building lot in Manor Park, a new development near "N" Division, Rockcliffe. We also chose the plan of the largest house of the three styles available, a roomy two-storey, priced at $8,500. I was happy that it would give us even more space than we'd had in our Toronto bungalow, and that, after the area was built up, everything would be quiet.

Bill was equally happy, and when he went back to work that afternoon at RCMP headquarters he told his immediate superior, Inspector George Archer, about his purchase.

"You'll had to withdraw from the deal," the inspector told Bill. "The commissioner has just ordered your transfer to Halifax as the Divisional Personnel Officer for the three maritime divisions and the Marine Section."

My spirits sank as I contemplated the upheaval of moving again. I might as well give up my book, even though my survival as an individual depended on my completing it. Bill seemed almost as desolate as I, and that evening we walked to a nearby movie theatre, hoping to take our minds off our worries. Danny Kaye, in *Wonder*

Man, soon had most of the audience rocking with laughter. But I sat stiff and silent, recoiling from each explosion of mirth that battered me beyond bearing. Long before the end of the movie Bill gently took my arm and led me home.

On Saturday morning the official word came: Bill would be transferred to Halifax at the end of the month. There was a police-rented house for us but it was up for sale.

The prospect of a house allowed us to rejoice in the move, and we blithely ignored the fact that it was up for sale. We anticipated further pleasure in Halifax because we now had a car, and Bill would be allowed to use it, on a mileage basis, for his travelling. As it was not a police car, nobody could object if I went with him from time to time. Suddenly life held hope.

Bill was allowed a week's holiday. We flew to Toronto to visit old friends and to buy furniture befitting what we had been told was a big house on a quiet residential street, perfect for an officer.

By the end of the week we had amassed all we needed. There were a chesterfield upholstered in white, grey, black and green tapestry, and a matching chair; a green occasional chair just right for my back and just right for contrast with our large print of the *Red* (rust) *Horses*; end tables and sectional bookcases of limed oak similar to our older bedroom suite. We also bought a limed-oak dining room suite with a sectional buffet and china cabinet, plus matching chairs upholstered in rough turquoise material. Finally, we indulged in two large East-Indian handmade rugs in soft beige-taupe for our living room and our separate dining room. These luxurious furnishings nearly depleted our bank account, but we told each other that the expense was well worth it, especially as the sectional pieces would fit in suitably wherever we might be transferred in future.

At last, after Bill's transfer had been postponed several times, we set out for Halifax in our own car, the first in our married life. I couldn't share in the driving because we had taken it for granted that Bill would teach me to drive and it hadn't worked out well. At the point where he'd been so concerned for the new Pontiac sedan that he had directed me in a choked whisper and had stiffened like a marble statue, I had willing agreed to withdraw from the lessons. Anyway, nothing mattered now except that we were heading for happiness.

TWENTY-FIVE

After I had wasted three weeks in the Nova Scotian hotel in Halifax, our furniture, old and new, arrived at 156 Henry Street. As Bill and I drove up to the big brown three-storey house, we found that a man and woman had followed the movers into the house. I took it as a good omen that friendly neighbours had come to welcome us. But they were the Presbyterian church choirmaster and his soloist wife. They wanted to get Bill for their tenor section before anyone else got him. Bill promised to sing solos from time to time, and the two left, beaming. But they were no happier than we as we settled into our new home.

Compared with the hell of Ottawa, Halifax was heaven. Granted, the house needed redecorating, but the outgoing inspector, Bill Nevin, and his wife had left it as clean as possible. The coal furnace would be a nuisance for me alone, but we'd find help somewhere. On the plus side, electricity heated the household hot water. Also, there was convenient space in the large kitchen for our washing machine.

Another advantage of 156 Henry Street was that four of its nine big rooms were available for me to choose one as my writing room. I took the brightest, on the second floor, and immediately set about finishing my RCMP history before the house was sold and we'd have to leave the perfect quiet of Henry Street.

A few days later we had one of many delightful experiences in the hospitable east-coast city. Mr. J.K. Hunter, an elderly neighbour, came to say he would buy the house if the police would continue to rent it. Bill made sure on that point, and the purchase was finalized. Then our new landlord, a semi-retired builder with a splendid reputation, offered to have the house completely redecorated. With gentle understanding he agreed to postpone the work till I had finished my book. The gods were indeed smiling on me!

For the next two months, except for two weeks, I wrote in peace almost every day, and often at night. But I took time out to find an osteopath, to make friends with the neighbours, and to go to church to hear Bill sing a solo each Sunday morning he was at home.

While I was finishing my book I allotted the minimum time to my household duties, although I cleaned and cooked and did laundry as necessary. Bill accused me of lacking housewifely pride. It upset him especially that our house, unlike all other houses on the street, had no glass curtains and thus the windows looked bare. So I left off writing for two weeks while I shopped for suitable material and made net curtains for the front door and for all the windows of the rooms on the first and second floors. Then once more I was free to concentrate on my reference books, RCMP *Quarterlies*, Annual Reports, and countless pages of notes. But now, in peace and quiet, I could remember everything.

On Saturday morning, June 12, I finished *The Men of the Mounted*, and immediately went out into the back yard to breathe in the fresh air and to bask in the sunshine. Two little girls left off playing next door and came over to visit.

"Why are you outside?" one of them asked.

"I've finished my work," I explained. "Why do you ask?"

"We thought you lived indoors all the time," the other one said.

That day in June 1948 marked the beginning of the happiest time of my married life to date. Mr. Hunter gave me a good start by calling in that afternoon and offering to let me choose how the house would be decorated. He couldn't have known what he might have been risking. In the home of one Mounted Police officer I had seen a wall at the end of a long dining room covered with vivid green wallpaper that was splashed with pink and red cabbage roses at least twelve inches in diameter. I'd heard of another Mounted Police home in which the walls and ceilings of two bedrooms had been painted red, to match the drapes and bedspreads.

My choice of decoration was much more conservative. I chose a creamy ivory paint for all the rooms, not only to show off our modern furniture but also because that colour would not clash with the furnishings of any future occupants. The wallpaper decorating the spacious front hall and leading up the stairway, however, needed no restraint. Bold rust and wine flowers and avocado-green leaves on a cream background gave life to the whole interior. And Mr. Hunter's most trusted painter showed his appreciation for countless cups of coffee and occasional friendly chats by refinishing the banister, in his own time and at his own expense, with a rich mahogany stain. It gleamed from his repeated gentle polishings, and set off the wallpaper to perfection. Looking about me at 156 Henry Street was almost as pleasant as listening to its silence.

Mr. Hunter, a widower, and his daughter and her family who lived with him, only two houses away from us, gave me pleasure in other ways. Daughter Faith Dewolfe, her husband, affectionately nicknamed Pooh but with no connection to Winnie of the same name, and their children Peter and Janie (later Jane), all welcomed the Kellys warmly. Before long they began inviting us to their cottage in the country. There Faith used to set the supper table with her homemade Boston baked beans and mustard pickles, both of which would have taken first prize in any contest.

Janie was one of the two little girls who had come over to see me the morning I had finished writing my book, and I was immediately fond of her. My heart ached when she started going to school in the fall and was classified as a blackbird because she couldn't sing in tune. I encouraged her to listen to the notes I played on the piano, notes at first widely separated, then gradually closer together. Before long she could distinguish between notes only a semitone apart. Then, by listening intently, she could sing what I played. So dear little Janie became a bluebird, and she and I became firm friends.

That same fall Mr. Hunter surprised us by having our coal furnace replaced by an oil-burning one, and I became more and more grateful to him.

I had seen the splendid houses he had built in the Henry Street area, and I admired him and enjoyed his company. After I got to know him better I sometimes visited him in the evenings when Bill was away. He was such an independent person that he refused to have a sitter when Faith and Pooh went out occasionally in the evening. But he was rather frail, and they were so concerned for his safety that they scarcely ever went out together. But I wasn't a sitter: I was a friend. So Faith and Pooh occasionally went out together, while Mr. Hunter and I thoroughly enjoyed each other's company. In fact, I grew so attached to Mr. Hunter and the Dewolfes that I felt I was part of a whole family, a feeling I hadn't had since I lived with the Johnson family at McLaren, Saskatchewan, almost two decades earlier.

Meanwhile, Bill worked incessantly and was away a lot. Now,

however, although I still loved him, I was happy without him, partly because I had matured past the point of longing for what I couldn't have. I accepted the fact that he must be away much of the time doing his DPO work at all RCMP detachments in Nova Scotia, New Brunswick and Prince Edward Island. I didn't fret that he would be at home only for interviews in Halifax, which was the headquarters not only of "H" Division (Nova Scotia), but also of the Marine Section. In fact, I accepted that his demanding work must take precedence over everything else.

After I had a milogram (a back X-ray with a spinal puncture and dye), that showed I would not benefit from an operation, it incapacitated me for three weeks with a Niagara Falls kind of headache. I was astounded that Bill postponed his travels till I had recovered. I accepted it as a matter of course when he was detailed for extra duties, as when he went to Hartford, Conneticut, for a week. In Hartford he spoke about Youth and the Police to various law enforcement leaders, and to groups of children that on one occasion numbered 3,000. While Bill was away I simply passed my time pleasantly at home.

On April 1, 1949, when Newfoundland joined Confederation and the RCMP took over its federal policing, Bill was given that tenth province as extra territory. But the Force could no longer surprise me.

Six months later the Canadian government agreed that the RCMP would also do Newfoundland's provincial policing on contract, as it did in certain other provinces. I still was not surprised that Bill was then constantly away for weeks at a time interviewing and setting up personnel files on the Newfoundland Rangers who automatically became members of the RCMP. It was also necessary for him to interview many members of the Newfoundland Constabulary so that a designated number of that police force could also become members of the RCMP. At least toward the end of this work he was assisted by a DPO inspector from western Canada. But he was still away from home for many weeks while travelling alone to many parts of Newfoundland and Labrador.

Although I regretted Bill's absence, I felt deep satisfaction that he was involved, even peripherally, with the entry of the former British colony into the Canadian Confederation. I had written a children's play about Dr. Wilfred Grenfell's work in Newfoundland and Labrador. My research had revealed the appalling truth about the hardships there. Impoverished fishermen had been forced to sell their fish to company stores at prices so low that they couldn't provide their families with even the most basic needs of food and clothing. Moreover, they had to buy those necessities from the same stores, at very high prices. Each poor fisherman, like the man in the song, could suitably have sung, "I owed my soul to the company store."

Bill's interviews with members of the police, a relatively privileged group, disclosed that even they were plagued by severe dental problems, and were endangered by tuberculosis. Bill, as I had been earlier, was shocked by what he learned. One elderly new Canadian's Old Age Security Pension provided him with more money than he had earned as a clerk in a company store while raising a family of six. And whereas in the past, mostly ragged clothing had hung from clotheslines, soon new clothes fluttered proudly in the Newfoundland breeze.

Each time Bill came home he seemed pleased to give me heartening news. I rejoiced that the Newfoundlanders had cast off the burden of colonialism, and that Canadian old-age pensions and family allowances would provide them with cash for life's necessities. I rejoiced too, that some old people now had cash to spend for the first time in their lives. And I felt a warm glow in knowing that Bill's usually cynical outlook didn't prevent him from feeling sympathy for oppressed fellow humans.

He was pleased to tell me that he had visited St. Anthony's, the headquarters of the Grenfell Mission on the northeast coast of Newfoundland. There he learned of the long-time splendid hospital facilities and medical services available for people of that northern area. The dedicated Dr. Thomas, then in charge of the mission, often travelled to outlying localities, mostly by boat to coastal points, but when necessary in winter by dog team to inland places.

No matter how busy Bill was with his DPO duties in Newfoundland and the Maritime provinces, he never neglected his secondary role as provider. He was always alert for delicacies to bring home. Fresh salmon, especially grilse, always scored a big hit with me. Lobsters, too, were most welcome, although I thought he had overdone it once when he brought home twenty-four live ones. Enthusiastically he took over the job of cooking them and removing the meat. But the freezing compartment of our small refrigerator held not much more than a few ice cubes, so we had to make sure we ate the lobster meat before it went bad. My mother, who was visiting us that summer, rebelled against lobster for breakfast. But Bill and I enjoyed it for three hearty meals a day as long as it lasted.

Fortunately it was during a cold November that he brought home a hundred pounds of oysters, so we kept them in a barrel outdoors. Eventually, however, we were forced to share them with friends and neighbours.

Only Bill's bargain sardines, two cartons of forty-eight tins each, failed to score well with me. They came from a small factory, and were of an unknown brand and not especially flavoursome. Even so, Bill and I ate them occasionally. Also, month after month I kept putting a few tins in each of the big food parcels we were still sending to Bill's parents. In spite of the continuing food scarcity in Great Britain, however, Mrs. Kelly eventually asked us not to send any more sardines.

Meanwhile, the publication of my book had been delayed because of continuing post-war paper shortages. At last, in October 1949, Dent managed to publish *The Men of the Mounted*. It received glowing reviews all across Canada, and *Time* magazine carried a few favourable inches about the book and its author. A Halifax radio station saluted me as "Woman of the Week" on the program "A Bouquet to You". But I came back to earth when the florist forgot to send my flowers and I had to telephone to remind him.

As usual I lacked any feeling of self-importance, but I was gratified to realize that in spite of all difficulties I had done what I set out to do.

I had told the Force's story, beginning with the earliest men and horses who trekked to the western prairies in 1874. I had written that some of them marched more than 1,900 miles, at first through mosquito-plagued heat of 100 degrees Farenheit, and finally through winter blizzards at 30 degrees below zero. I had told about men who had saved settlers from prairie fires. I had told about men and horses who, on government orders, had spent several desperate years hacking out a wilderness trail to nowhere.

With heavy heart I told the story of thirty-two-year-old Margaret Clay, who had been ravaged by husky dogs while her husband was away on a northern patrol. She had had one leg amputated by a priest and a Hudsons' Bay Company factor, assisted by two constables. Nevertheless, she had died before her husband returned.

I had also told the story of the modern mounties and their dedication, with highlights such as the Gold Case, in spite of Bill's prohibition of my putting him into the book.

Reviewers praised the book as "highly readable", and I knew that, within the limits of the accuracy of my research material, I had made it factual. Best of all, I was acknowledged as a writer, a worthy individual.

Unfortunately, I didn't do as well in getting publicity as I had done in writing the book. By contrast with present-day authors, I failed to realize the importance of publicity. I didn't want to be the personal focus of attention, and I presumed that any publicity would come through the splendid reviews or by way of Dent. I gave a talk to the Women's Canadian Club, but I talked as much about my difficulties in writing *The Men of the Mounted* as about the history it contained. That of course was a grave mistake. Then a nurses' organization asked me to talk to them, and I declined.

At that point the Men's Canadian Club invited Bill to talk to them about the history of the Force. Instead of my being upset at what I might have considered male discrimination, I was relieved that Bill was the one to give the talk. I was equally relieved that no other organization invited me to appear in public.

I was very upset, however, when my application to join the Canadian Authors Association was rejected. I'd been confident of acceptance. Members of the Halifax branch of the CAA had welcomed me and had allowed me to attend their meetings as a guest. Moreover, I'd been writing book reviews regularly for Will R. Bird, president of the Halifax branch and an established author (*Here Lies Good Yorkshire*). He gave me the assignment of reviewing all books he didn't want to review himself, and my reviews appeared with his in one of the area's weekly newspapers.

Naturally I was shocked at being rejected by the CAA. I was even more shocked at the reason for the rejection: that I had plagiarized the work of one its members. It was true that I had used Mrs. T.'s book on the RCMP schooner *St. Roch* as one of my reference books. But I had based my account of *St. Roch*'s sailing through the North West Passage almost entirely on RCMP official records and newspaper and magazine articles. However, I had felt I needed a few anecdotes to brighten my account, and I wanted to use five short ones from Mrs. T.'s book. I had explained to my editor, Mr. Eustace, that the five anecdotes would be the only parts of my whole book that I couldn't verify, and I asked his advice as to whether or not I should use them.

Mr. Eustace had replied that as Mrs. T.'s book was reputedly authentic history, the incidents must be true. I could use them, but in different words. I had followed his advice.

At the same time as Mrs. T. tried to keep me from joining the CAA, she threatened to sue Dent for plagiarism. Mr. Eustace asked me to check with Henry Larsen, the skipper who had taken the *St. Roch* through the North West Passage, to learn if the incidents were actually true. Bill and I went to Ottawa to see Larsen, and explained to him why it was so important for me to know. But no matter how I questioned him, he steadfastly refused to tell me, perhaps because he was afraid he might be involved in a lawsuit. Then Mrs. T.

declared she had "created" the five incidents for added human interest in her book. Dent paid her an out-of-court settlement. Fortunately for me, Will R. Bird explained the truth to the CAA executive and I was allowed to join.

Several years later I attended a CAA convention which Mrs. T. also attended. I had always regretted what I believed must be her misunderstanding of the situation, and I stopped her in the hall to explain. She refused to listen. I followed her into a washroom and blocked her way out. Then I apologized for having used her material, and explained that it wasn't really my fault.

"Oh, I knew that all the time!" she snapped.

I left her without another word.

Mrs. T. was strikingly different from all the other writers I knew. I had kept in touch with my Toronto writer friends, and they had all shown pleasure in the publication of *The Men of the Mounted*. The members of the Halifax branch of the CAA, who in addition to Will R. Bird included such notables as folklorist Helen (later Dr.) Creighton; world-affairs expert Dr. Stewart; novelist-historian Thomas Raddall, warmly welcomed me as a fellow member. When before long I instigated the formation of a writers' workshop like the Pen Guild in Toronto, their friendship seemed even warmer.

Although I didn't immediately begin another book, I continued to write and sell smaller things, enjoying everything I did in the peace and quiet of Henry Street. I had bought an IBM electric typewriter, one of the first produced by the company. It allowed me to work much faster than before. In fact, it took me only three weeks to write a 100-page workbook for School Publications, to go with the new Grade 5 reader. If I had used my little old portable, the project would have taken me two months.

Everything was going splendidly! I felt happier than ever to be living in Halifax among friends, and writing contentedly in the hush of dear Henry Street.

Summer, 1948, Halifax. Five-year-old Janie DeWolfe, right, and her friend Susan in front of 156 Henry Street. They saw me in the back garden the morning I finished writing The Men of the Mounted. *They thought I lived indoors, and wanted to know why I was outside.*

1948, Vancouver. My mother had retired from teaching and was living in Vancouver. She had just won a radio contest, the prizes being her hairdo, the orchid and the photography session.

1949, Halifax. This photo was used on the jacket of my first RCMP history, The Men of the Mounted.

1948, Halifax. Bill is sitting in our first car, in front of 156 Henry Street

TWENTY-SIX

On the sunny afternoon of May 29, 1950 Bill and I joined a group of Mounted Police people and other well-wishers who had assembled at the Halifax docks. We were there to welcome the *St. Roch* as it sailed into the harbour and docked at one of the wharves. Pennants fluttered in the breeze, harbour craft whistle or tooted, people clapped or cheered, reporters scribbled in notebooks, and photographers snapped pictures. Everyone was acknowledging that as the little schooner sailed into the harbour it had earned the distinction of being the first ship to sail completely around the North American continent.

I gazed with awe and admiration at the 104-foot, two-masted, power-equipped schooner that until then I had known only through reading. As many of us knew, it had been built of ironwood for strength against Arctic ice. Since 1928 the RCMP had used it as a northern detachment, in summer floating and mobile, and in winter stationary, frozen in the Arctic ice. Now it had made the first ever circumnavigation of North America!

That achievement was only one of the *St. Roch*'s claims to fame. In October 1942, after three years of devastating world war, the RCMP announced that Skipper (Staff Sergeant) Henry Larsen and his small crew had successfully fought a twenty-eight-month battle against the stark forces of nature in Arctic waters. That historic voyage, the Canadian public learned, had begun in June 1940, with absolutely no publicity. During the voyage Larsen and his men had sailed almost 10,000 miles, sometimes fighting their way inch by inch, from Vancouver to Halifax through the treacherous Northwest Passage. Their purpose was to indicate that the territory north of the Canadian mainland was Canadian.

Their perilous, often almost fatal voyage in Arctic waters had taken them from west to east through the southern route of the Passage, travelled before only by Roald Amundsen in 1903-1906, in his sailing sloop *Gjoya*. Larsen and his men, always alert to danger, and often sleepless night after day after night, had faced terrible gales, threatening ice floes, and innumerable other northern hazards. But their successful voyage had done what the Canadian government had hoped it would do: it proclaimed to the world that our Arctic waters were indeed Canadian.

In 1944, Henry Larsen again skippered the *St. Roch* through the Northwest Passage. This time, however, as it sailed from Halifax back to Vancouver, it travelled the northern route of the Passage. Again Larsen and his crew battled gales, fog, snow, ice floes and icebergs, but this time they made the journey in only one season. Thus they were the first to sail through the northern route and the first to sail either way through the Passage in one season. Also, the *St. Roch* was the only ship to have sailed through the Northwest Passage in both directions. Even more important was that the RCMP had re-enforced Canada's claim to the Canadian Arctic.

By 1950 Henry Larsen had been promoted to Inspector Larsen and had become OC of the northern "G" Division. So when the *St. Roch* left Vancouver and headed south, beginning a voyage back to Halifax by way of the Panama Canal, Larsen had been succeeded by Inspector Ken Hall as skipper. But as the little ship sailed into Halifax harbour on that sunny afternoon in late May of that year, the welcoming crowd honoured all the men who had shared in those achievements, and the RCMP schooner that had served them so well. As Inspector Hall stood on the bridge with his wife, who had been ferried out to meet him, they waved acknowledgement of the crowd's warm welcome, probably feeling as proud as we felt.

Only one of the Northwest Passage crew members, Sergeant F.S. Farrar, had sailed completely around the North American continent. Pestered by reporters wanting to know how he felt, he shrugged off any credit.

"Had I done it alone, by canoe," he wrote later, "I might have boasted a little."

That attitude was typical of almost all the Mounted Police I knew. They seemed to take for granted their own exploits and those of their fellow mounties, on land or sea.

Land-based Inspector M., however, failed to appreciate the work of the Marine Section. Soon after we had welcomed the *St. Roch* at the end of its great voyage, he was transferred from his position as OC of a sub/division of "H" Division. He had always given the impression that only his unique ability had enabled him to guide the affairs of that sub/division. It irked him that his replacement, at least temporarily, would be the Marine Section's Inspector Hall, who had had land training but little police experience.

"Oh, hell!" Inspector M. said glumly as he bade Bill and me goodbye. "What's a sub/division when it can be taken over like this by a bloody sailor!"

By contrast, I admired the members of the Marine Section for their skill, dedication and bravery in both peacetime and wartime. Bill liked and admired them, too, and always got along as well with the Marine members as with the other mounties. So when the wife of one Marine officer invited us to her Saturday evening Musicale and asked us to bring our music, of course we accepted. We simply ignored the warning of a land-based officer that some Marine officers and their navy pals partied with abandon every Saturday night.

We arrived for the Musicale rather late, and found no sign of abandonment or revelry. But we did notice that the party room was clouded with cigarette smoke, and we were immediately aware of the strong fumes of alcoholic beverages. Apparently the other guests had arrived much earlier.

"Hurry up!" one of them shouted. "Have a drink and let's start the music. That's what we came for."

Alcohol makes me stupid, so usually the only drink I have is a small sherry. But there wasn't any sherry. There were only rum and whiskey, sailor fashion. So I had no choice but to set myself apart from the rest of the crowd by asking for a ginger ale. A man immediately put it on the piano, as if I were expected to drink and play without delay.

I played for community singing, mostly sailor songs and sea shanties. It was lucky that I knew them, as no one had provided any music for those songs. Next Bill sang whatever he chose. Soon the other guests were shouting praise and encouragement, and demanding their favourites. After an hour of continuous singing, Bill was tired and gave up. Meanwhile the others had been sitting drinking. Now they wanted more community singing.

"I'm as tired as Bill," I protested, with more good humour than I felt. Then I turned to the hostess. "Who would have provided the music if we hadn't come?" I asked. "Let's give someone else a chance."

A short stocky man, not a Marine member but a civilian friend, eagerly took over at the piano. Apparently he, too, could play without music. Unfortunately, he could play in only two keys, C and G. Listening to his right hand melody wasn't too disturbing, although mostly he used one finger only, like a hammer. His pom-pomming of the bass, however, was much worse. He used only two chords, the C and G tonic triads, and he thumped them indiscriminantly. The other guests, far along in their drinking, sang at the top of their voices, apparently carried away by the glorious fortissimos they and the pianist were directing heavenward.

I, on the other hand, felt panicky at being trapped in their cacophony. It reminded me of *The Musicians of Bremen*, in which a donkey, a rooster, a dog and a cat formed a "band" and made ear-splitting sounds that frightened away would-be robbers. In self defence I offered to take over the piano again.

The hostess brought in trays of appetizing sandwiches and went back to the kitchen for more goodies. The choristers immediately attacked the food, eating and singing at the same time. None of them passed anything to me, perhaps because that might have cut off my contribution. But I soon stopped playing, joking that I, too, was hungry.

Then the hostess, a sweet, gentle, soft-spoken woman who seemed out of place at her own party, aimed for general sociability at lunch time by designating partners. Unfortunately, my partner wanted to keep on singing. He and the two-key, two-chord man provided nonstop background music. Meanwhile the rest of us enjoyed the delicious sandwiches and the melt-in-the-mouth lemon pie, better than any I had tasted since I lived with the Johnson family at McLaren. Bill, the only notably sober man there, found himself looking after two women partners because the partner of one of them refused to stop singing. And, of course, Bill also looked after me part of the time.

"More shinging!" my non-partner shouted immediately after lunch.

The other choristers, presumably having gained their second wind, agreed vociferously.

"But firsht, letsh have shome opera!" one of them shouted.

I went to the piano, but I whispered to Bill that I wouldn't play opera for these people who couldn't possibly appreciate it.

"Then make some excuse," Bill muttered.

Looking round the room, I chuckled my most companionable chuckle. "So sorry," I smiled. "Bill has eaten too much lunch to sing opera. You should have asked earlier. He will sing only two more songs."

After those two I declined to play any longer, even though I had to endure the two-key, two-chord man's heavy hammering and discordant pom-pomming until the party ended. Anyway, as I realized later, not once during that Musicale evening did anybody discuss Mounted Police affairs.

Strangely enough, the Musicale turned out to be well worth while for me personally, although I didn't follow Bill's suggestion that we in turn should give a Musicale. Instead I made friends with the hostess of that earlier one. During the infrequent lulls at her party, she and I had discovered that we had much in common. Later, while our husbands were away, I spent many hours enjoying her delightful company. I also had the pleasure of getting to know her two small daughters, and being favoured occasionally with a large slice of Canada's best lemon pie.

During our three years in Halifax I formed so many warm friendships that I would have liked to stay there forever. Many of those friends also became, though briefly, friends of my mother. In the summer of 1950, when she holidayed with us and when the national body of the CAA held its annual convention in Halifax, Mom and Bill attended all social functions as my guests. Members of the Halifax branch welcomed Mom with the old-world courtesy for which many older Haligonians were noted. Both she and I were touched and I felt grateful. Some of the wives of the Mounted Police officers also made a fuss over her, as did Mr. Hunter and his family. In fact, my friends in Halifax made that city my best home to date.

Meanwhile, in spite of Bill's overwork, he and I had made the most of our limited time together, with friends, occasional concerts and art exhibitions. Also, we sometimes drove in our own car to Herring Cove, Peggy's Cove, Lunenberg, and scores of other picturesque places on the Nova Scotia coast. One fall we spent a week in New York City, enjoying our first visit there. Resolutely we crammed in all possible ballets, musical dramas, art galleries, museums and an opera.

At home in Halifax, because Bill still sang with pleasure whenever and wherever he was invited, we spent whatever time we could with music. Also, during two winter seasons we studied painting at the Nova Scotia College of Art. Bill was keen on learning to paint, but wouldn't use his spare time to go to classes without me, so I went, too. That led us to new friends – classmates, our favourite teacher and his wife, and a talented woman who not only painted well in oils, but also played the harp.

No wonder I wanted to stay in Halifax, living on a quiet street, in a beautifully decorated, convenient and spacious house, surrounded by more friends than I would have believed possible. As we began to hear rumours of Bill's possible transfer, my sympathy went out to the four-year-old daughter of the OC of "H" Division. That officer's transfer to Halifax had been the second within a year, and at each move the little girl had reluctantly left her friends behind. When her mother asked her what she would like for her fifth birthday, she looked ready to cry.

"What I want most," she sniffled, "is for daddy not to get transferred before my birthday."

In spite of my reluctance to leave Halifax, when Bill learned early in 1951 that we were going to be transferred in a few months, I rejoiced. We were going to Fredericton, an attractive university city on the banks of the beautiful St. John river. Bill would be the OC of Fredericton sub/division, which took in about half of the small "J" Division (New Brunswick). He would be responsible for supervising the work of all the detachments in his district, but would be at home most of the time.

Perhaps there would even be time for us to stroll along the bank of the St. John river as we used to stroll along the bank of the North Saskatchewan river in our North Battleford days. Perhaps at last, after more than a decade of the unsettling demands of Bill's work, we could enjoy a normal married life. What happiness! And what peace of mind for me! I would begin my next book as soon as we were well settled in Fredericton.

We even had a house to go to, one that would be left vacant by the inspector who was exchanging positions with Bill. We felt sure it would be an attractive home, since when we proudly escorted Inspector C. over our pleasantly decorated, immaculately clean house, he said that the house he was leaving was in much the same condition.

I didn't trust Inspector C. A senior officer had told Bill that he'd had "the unprecedented gall" to scheme, but unsuccessfully, to have the new RCMP stove at his Fredericton house transferred with him to Halifax. That new one would replace the rather decrepit one that belonged with our house. If he had succeeded, we would have had to take our worn-out stove to Fredericton. Even so, I saw no reason for Inspector C. to lie about the condition of his house.

After our many Halifax friends had entertained us royally, and the movers had done all the packing and had loaded their big van, we spent a night at the Lord Nelson hotel. At breakfast, by courtesy of Bill's expense account, I celebrated with a large shrimp cocktail. Then, smiling with contentment, we set out in our black Pontiac sedan, bound for Fredericton and a happy home life.

TWENTY-SEVEN

We arrived at 416 University Avenue, Fredericton, at exactly noon on Wednesday, April 18, 1951, and saw our mover's truck parked near that semi-detached house. The C.'s movers' had gone for lunch before loading their truck, so ours had to wait. Indoors we found Mrs. C. in the kitchen, wandering about in a daze among the displaced furniture and the piles of cartons and boxes. She was carrying the head of a dust mop, shaking it nervously. Wherever she went, it dropped balls of fuzz among the heaps of clothing and the still-damp washing spread on chairs to dry.

Bill had to report to the OC of the division, so he left me to inspect our new home alone. Mrs. C. led me past the sink heaped with empty bottles, bottoms and tops of empty chocolate boxes, smelly rags and cigarette butts. We moved on, past the rose-coloured sweater hanging to dry in a doorway, and on to the other main-floor rooms.

Perhaps my expression showed Mrs. C. how shocked I was to see the grime on the walls that made the house look like a slum.

"The coal furnace exploded about a year ago," she explained. "The landlady didn't redecorate."

Upstairs I saw that the bedrooms had not escaped the blast, and that the floors of the clothes closets were littered with broken dress hangers and balls of dust-fluff.

Feeling nauseated, I left Mrs. C. and stood outside in the fresh air. There I waited until Bill came back to take me to lunch and to allow Mrs. C. and her movers time to leave.

After lunch, while Bill and I supervised our movers, we made other devastating discoveries. Dust balls remained where the refrigerator had stood. Blobs of sticky syrup oozed along the pantry shelf. Rat droppings clustered under the gratings of the cold air registers on the main floor. Even the oven of the nearly-new electric stove, which was the only thing in good condition and which Inspector C. had schemed to take with him, had a great heap of gray ashes from burned food never wiped up.

The bathroom was in no better condition than the rest of the house, and the lid of the toilet tank, broken in half, lay on the floor. The kitchen ceiling, directly under the bathroom, had great chunks of loose plaster. It looked as if the toilet or the bath had overflowed, and had seeped down and loosened the plaster.

The back kitchen, which looked like an old woodshed, housed a hot-water tank that was heated by kerosene. That liquid had to be poured into a container on the side of the heater from a very large, very heavy glass jug. I couldn't possibly lift the jug from the rickety wooden crate on which it sat precariously.

Our movers carried in our furniture, one beautiful piece after another, and I locked myself in the bathroom and wept.

By two o'clock that afternoon Bill and I had decided to buy a house in the nearby development of Sunshine Gardens, and Bill planned to advise the RCMP to break their lease on the semi-detached slum. Until we left for Sunshine Gardens, we knew we couldn't bear to live where the C.s had lived, at least not until the worst of the dirt was cleaned up. So we drove to the Lord Beaverbrook Hotel and checked in. Later Bill dropped me off at the house, so that I could begin the cleaning. He went to the office to take over as OC of Fredericton sub/division from Inspector C., who had not yet left the city.

The first time I flushed the toilet, the tank didn't refill. By this time, however, my nausea had given way to anger – at the RCMP in general and at the C.s in particular. I would not be beaten by those despicable creatures! I took off the two halves of the tank lid that I'd just tidied up from the floor, and peered in. As I'd never before experienced trouble with a toilet tank, I couldn't tell what was wrong. I got the filler hose from our washing machine and attached it to the cold water tap of the wash basin. But when I turned on the tap, the water leaked out. And as I leaned over to adjust it, a sudden squirt hit me in the eye. I still didn't intend to be beaten by the RCMP or the C.s, but I left the toilet fixing for Bill.

He found that the arm holding the floater bulb caught on the overflow pipe every time the tank was filled. Hence after each flushing the tank lid had to be lifted and the floater bulb jiggled loose. When Bill tried to fix it by bending the floater arm, the arm broke. Then the water ran and wouldn't stop.

The next day a plumber told us that the only way he could stop it was to take out the whole toilet, take up the floor, and put in all new pipes. He warned us that any hammering in the bathroom would bring down the plaster ceiling in the kitchen underneath. I couldn't face the extra mess, so we decided to let the water run till we moved to the house we intended to buy. Later I learned that, three years earlier, Mrs. C. had become fed up with having to take off the tank lid every time she flushed the toilet. One day she slammed the lid against the tank. It broke in two, and the pieces, I presumed, had lain on the bathroom floor ever since.

Meanwhile, on that first Wednesday at 416 University Avenue, I worked hard all afternoon. Bill and I worked hard all evening. I was at it again the next day, Thursday. But considering everything that must be done, we had accomplished practically nothing. On Friday, at Bill's request, two RCMP janitors worked all day, and on Saturday a private cleaning woman worked all day. Even then there was a lot still to be done.

On Monday Bill and I moved from the elegant Lord Beaverbrook to the hovel we must call home, at least for the time being. On Tuesday the two RCMP janitors put in another full day's work, and on Wednesday my cleaning woman came again.

By this time, whatever could be cleaned had been cleaned, including all cold air registers, and Bill and I prepared to put up with the situation as best we could. I was afraid, though, that even without any hammering in the bathroom, the kitchen ceiling would drop its loose plaster on my head as I stood at the kitchen sink or the stove. I wanted Bill to get a construction worker's hard hat for me. But he was annoyed that someone might see me wearing it. So I merely did as little work as possible in the kitchen.

I also wanted Bill, or the officer in charge of rentals, or the OC of the New Brunswick Division, who was also stationed in Fredericton, to put in a detailed report against Inspector C. I wanted somebody to make sure that he would never again leave a police-rented house in such repulsive condition.

I don't know if it was the officers' esprit-de-corps that kept all those concerned from reporting the shocking truth and thus possibly protecting other wives from what I'd had to face. In any case, not one of them took up the challenge on behalf of officers' wives, and all of them, including Bill, dropped to rock bottom in my estimation. Obviously we wives, like the constables and NCOs, needed a personnel department to help relieve our troubles.

Meanwhile, on Friday two days after we arrived in Fredericton, Bill and I had made definite arrangements to buy a house to be built in Sunshine Gardens. At that time only the basement had been constructed, so the builder gave me the plans and said I could make changes if I did so within the next few days. I was grateful for the opportunity. He set me up with large sheets of blueprint paper and white pencils, and showed me exactly how to draw a revised set of plans.

The day after we moved from the Lord Beaverbrook into 416 University Avenue I set to work, ignoring the two janitors also working there that day. On the next day, Wednesday, my cleaning woman worked all day, but I also ignored her and took time out only to make her lunch. On Thursday I had the day alone, and I finished the plans.

My system had worked well. First I measured the length and width of all our main pieces of furniture and the rugs, and then cut out cardboard rectangles to scale. Next I arranged them on the various room plans to best advantage, and changed the position of windows, cupboards, and even doors as necessary. At last I redrew the plans, with all new measurements marked in exactly the same way as the old measurements were indicated on the original blueprints. It was the first time I'd done such a thing, so it had taken me three days. But I felt it was worth all the effort. On Thursday evening the builder accepted my plans, and on Friday morning, April 27, I relaxed and visualized a happy future.

On Monday, April 30, the last day I needed my cleaning woman for the time being, we learned that Commissioner Wood, whose term of office had been extended after the death of Deputy Commissioner Gagnon, had retired. Simultaneously we learned that Assistant Commissioner L.H. Nicholson would succeed him, but we didn't expect that to affect us.

Nevertheless, on Tuesday morning, May 1, Superintendent Perlson, OC of New Brunswick Division, called Bill into his office. He said that Commissioner Nicholson had just telephoned to say he wanted to see Bill in Ottawa the next morning, but Perlson didn't know why.

On Wednesday morning Bill flew to Ottawa. I spent the same morning unpacking the last of our trunks and distributing their contents anywhere I felt was clean enough to receive them.

That evening I settled myself in bed, waiting for a call on the extension telephone installed earlier that day for my convenience.

Closing my eyes to shut out the filthy wallpaper we had not been able to clean, I listened to the CBC Wednesday Night program on astronomy. Then came the expected call from Bill. It dealt me what was almost a knockout blow.

We were to be transferred!

Commissioner Nicholson wanted us to go to London, England, for two years, during which Bill would travel over most of Europe. Nicholson had suggested that Bill should discuss it with me before making up his mind about going.

After a deathly silence I asked, "What did you tell him?"

"I said we'd go," Bill replied enthusiastically. "The work will be an exciting change. What do you think?"

What did it matter what I thought? Anyway, how could I admit to Bill, that I believed that he, too, had wanted more than anything to have the settled home life we had almost achieved? How could I express my dismay in realizing that he still put his exciting work above everything and everyone?

Did Commissioner Nicholson really expect me to say I didn't want to go? And what if I did say so?

Somewhere in my mind was a letter I'd come across in my research. It was written to a mountie's wife who'd had the temerity to write to her husband's commissioner complaining about a transfer. The year was 1927, and the commissioner was Cortlandt Starnes. Earlier that same year he had raised the currently needed seven years of premarriage service to eight years for NCOs and twelve years for constables. On the occasion of receiving Mrs. Blank's letter, written without her husband's knowledge, Commissioner Starnes, like Queen Victoria before him, was not amused. His reply, dated November 11, 1927, made that point very clear.

> Dear Mrs. Blank,
> I have received your note, dated the 13th of last month, with a great deal of regret . . . Your action in writing to me, as you did, has made a very bad impression upon me, and I am wondering if the spirit of the Force is not deteriorating . . . It seems no one wants to go anywhere except in the height of comfort . . .
> The contrast offered by Mrs. X, Mrs. Y, and a good many others, including my own wife, comes to mind. These ladies in proceeding to the same post as you are going, spent three months in camp, and endured a walk of 175 miles over the mountains. These officers' wives prided themselves on this fact and we heard no complaints.

I am . . . answering you direct, and leave it to you as to
whether you will show (your husband) my answer or
not.
Yours sincerely,
Cortlandt Starnes

As for my complaining, it should not be to the commissioner,
but to Bill. I was shocked into silence.

"Well?" I heard Bill saying impatiently, "What do you think?"

"What does it matter what I think?" I replied hopelessly.

"Anyway," Bill said, "surely you see how I feel?"

"I see," I faltered, too battered even to weep, and soon I hung up.

Falling back against the pillow, I felt the room swirling about me.
After a time, I didn't know how long, I switched the radio on again
and forced myself to listen again to the astronomy program.
Somehow it comforted me to know there was something out there I
could count on. Never mind about people. At least the planets, the
solar system, the galaxy, the stars, the whole universe, were as reliable as anything ever could be. Even from energy to matter and back
was reliable. Even if $E=mc^2$ was all there was to everything, it was
still something to hold on to.

Whatever it was, something kept me from collapsing that night.
Eventually I pushed the coming transfer from my mind and fell
asleep.

The nightmare came later, by day. First we had to cancel our application to buy the house in Sunshine Gardens, along with my plans
for a settled home life and happiness there. Then we learned that we
had to vacate our University Avenue house in three weeks for Bill's
successor, although we didn't know when we'd be leaving for
England. We did know that we'd go first to Ottawa, where Bill would
be briefed on his new work, and where we'd stay until berths on a
ship were available. We knew, too, that we'd stay in a hotel in
London until we found living accommodation. But we didn't know
how long we'd be in any one place. And although we knew that we
couldn't take our furniture, we didn't know what few household
things we should take.

Fredericton had no furniture storage company, but we found a
place in Moncton, undesirable but somewhat better than the only
other, impossible, one. We drove to St. John to buy wardrobe trunks
and extra suitcases. While we were waiting to leave Fredericton, Bill
still sang at local churches whenever he was invited, so I had to practice with him in spite of my inner turmoil.

There was turmoil in our house, too. We ended up with everything sorted into groups. In one place lay the clothing we must take with us for several weeks in Ottawa and for the voyage. In another place we set aside our clothing to be shipped with us for an unknown time in a London hotel. Also set aside to be shipped, but which must be kept separate because we'd need those things only after we found a house in England, was a great heap of most-used cooking utensils, bed linen, blankets, pillows, towels, my IBM electric typewriter in a crate obligingly supplied by the nearest IBM service man, and a few books I couldn't bear to leave behind. Whatever was left would, of course, go into storage in Moncton.

Bill sold the car, and I took extra chiropractic treatments. He escaped to the office most of the time, while I stayed at home with the soot-grimed wallpaper, the water running in the toilet, the loose plaster on the kitchen ceiling, the kerosene fumes in the back kitchen, and the piles of clothing and household goods.

The worst thing for me to put up with was the blaring radio music that came hour after hour through the flimsy common wall of the semi-detached dwellings. The woman next door was a pleasant, friendly neighbour. When I admired her beautiful hands, she generously offered me her secret recipe for the hand lotion she made herself. Unfortunately, she was deaf. At our first meeting she had explained that the only way she could have a normal life was with top volume from her husband, friends, radio and phonograph. How could I protest when all she wanted was as normal a life as possible?

Other unwelcome sounds adding to my turmoil came from the university about two hundred yards up the hill. It had been heavily endowed by Lord Beaverbrook, and university officials honoured their patron by playing his favourite song on the chimes of the clock in the university tower. Bits of "The Jones Boys" rang out, loud and clear, every fifteen minutes, with a longer arrangement every hour on the hour. I wanted to scream at the Chinese-torture repetitions.

The confusion was almost more than I could bear, and my whole being ached to escape. I had a glimpse of what was happening to me as I handled an unfinished summer dress I had been making just before we left Halifax. The pretty dress, pink with a black and gray scroll design, still needed a fair amount of machine sewing, and of course I'd had no chance to do it in Fredericton. Now I held the unfinished dress, staring first at it, then at one pile of clothing after another, unable to decide in which pile it belonged.

Suddenly I heard myself shrieking, "Put it in a box! Put it in a box!" as if that would solve the problem. Then I broke down and wept hopelessly. As I fought to regain my composure, I felt vaguely that the box symbolized a coffin.

Somehow I kept my sanity and survived. On May 30, exactly six weeks from the day we had arrived in Fredericton, we moved from the confusion of 416 University Avenue to the tranquility of the Lord Beaverbrook hotel. Two days later we moved on again, to Ottawa and the Lord Elgin hotel. After three stifling June weeks there, without air conditioning in those days, we moved on once more, to Montreal and the *Empress of France*, en route to London, England.

TWENTY-EIGHT

As Bill and I settled ourselves comfortably in our first-class cabin on the *Empress of France*, I accepted the fact that the shocking transfer to England was merely part of what I had contracted for, though unknowingly, when I became a mountie's wife and camp follower. I would not let regret over my lost chance of a settled, companionable life in Fredericton overwhelm me. I would accept Bill's new job as vitally important, just as I had accepted his wartime work and his DPO travels.

His new job was indeed important. He would be in charge of Visa Control operations in most of Europe west of the USSR's "iron curtain". Since the end of World War II in 1945, hundreds of thousands of displaced persons, mainly from behind the iron curtain, wanted to obtain visas allowing them to emigrate to more desirable homelands, including Canada. Since 1946, members of the RCMP had been stationed in various European cities, and had conducted security checks on visa applicants. They advised Canadian immigration officials, also stationed in Europe, as to the security status of those would-be immigrants. This helped immigration officials decide which applicants should be granted visas.

The Mounted Police and their Visa Control operations had been loosely supervised by a retired RCMP superintendent living near London. But Commissioner Nicholson realized that stricter supervision was necessary. Bill would provide that supervision, and would set up additional RCMP offices as necessary. He would also have a second job, an important first in RCMP history. He would be the liaison officer between the RCMP and most European security, intelligence, and police organizations in his vast territory.

Obviously he would be away from home much of the time, so I must compensate somehow. I decided to spend my two years in England by learning everything I could about the country and its people, and by immersing myself in its culture. I would return home better educated than when I left.

My education began during my first lunch on the *Empress of France*: passengers on British steamships still felt the effects of postwar shortages. The main ingredient of the clam chowder seemed to be lukewarm water, with no milk or butter. The salad consisted of a wilted leaf of lettuce, a slice of soggy tomato, three limp shreds of carrot, a bow-shaped slice of beetroot, with no dressing, not even oil and vinegar. It was served on a kidney-shaped side plate, and reminded me of what a nurse held under the chin of a nauseated patient during the upheaval. We also had rolls but no butter. My choice of dessert, black currant pie, had such hard crust, presumably from the reduction of fat, that I couldn't eat it. The filling seemed almost devoid of sugar, but I was so hungry that I ate it anyway.

Bill optimistically chose a chocolate eclair. It was soggy from the gelatine filling, and the "chocolate" topping was a small sprinkling of sugar and cocoa. There was no cream for coffee, only warm milk, and there was no milk for adult passengers to drink.

"And this," I whispered to Bill, "is first-class food!"

My education progressed as we sat in our deck chairs after lunch. We had queued for the chairs and their positions, so we had no choice of companions. On my left sat the Archbishop of Liverpool in what I presumed was his finest clerical garb. Bill sat on my right, and on his right sat the stocky Sir Frank Pratt, then his plump wife, Lady Pratt. I thought what luck it was to have an archbishop and a titled couple as neighbours. I expected to have fascinating items to record in my oversize notebook.

The items were not what I had anticipated. The archbishop politely initiated a conversation about the quality of the lunch, but at the same time Sir Frank began shouting something at Bill. The archbishop tried in vain to out-shout Sir Frank. Soon he struggled out of the low-slung deck chair and hurried away, never again to sit beside me.

As I turned my attention to what Sir Frank was shouting, I was amazed to notice the knight's accent. I had learned a lot about English accents, both from my early life in England and from the comments of my English relatives over the years. I placed his origin as northern England, perhaps Lancashire. He was telling Bill that he had been knighted because his cotton mills produced great quantities of much-needed cotton goods during the war, and the government was grateful.

"I deserved it, by gum," he proclaimed. "During the war I was proposed for knighthood four or five times before they (the Conservative government) accepted me. I finally made it, but only after the chairman of a certain committee was replaced."

Sir Frank was specially pleased to tell us that the magazine *Punch* had published a cartoon of him and had called him "a spinner of coarse yarns."

He had benefitted in other ways, too, from the scarcity of consumer goods in wartime. He didn't tell us how many cotton mills he had to start with, but during the next few days he gave us full details of his present worth. He had fifty-three cotton mills, a twelve-acre place with four acres in gardens, two gardeners, and three cars, including a Packard. He had a chauffeur, a butler, a housekeeper, a cook and several maids. He also owned a huge grand piano that no one in his family could play. In fact, his twenty-seven-year-old daughter listened to the radio all day, with the mindless music so loud that Sir Frank couldn't stand it. No, it didn't bother him when he wanted to read. He read books only on sea voyages, and then only mystery novels.

Of course there were other diversions on board the *Empress of France*. We had the usual bingos and movies. We also had daily horse races in which cut-out "horses" moved forward according to throws of dice. But Lady Pratt said it was too much trouble to walk from our deck chairs to where a steward was taking bets about fifty yards away.

We had the customary cocktails with the captain, and a visit to the bridge, dancing and a musical evening. We saw an iceberg, and the ship circled a dead whale to give passengers a good look at it.

Occasionally Sir Frank let his wife relate her experiences. We learned that she sometimes drove forty miles to Liverpool, hoping to get two grapefruit. And once she arrived home with two dozen!

"The dockers didn't want them," she explained. "They wanted red meat." So I presumed that the dockers opened a sealed shipping crate and stole the contents, which turned out not to be red meat but grapefruit.

Lady Pratt also obtained luxury foods from her grocer.

"But I never ask what he has hidden at the bottom of my shopping bag, or the exhorbitant prices he hides in my monthly accounts," she said.

"Of course the tradesmen stick us," Sir Frank chuckled. "But what can we do? Sometimes under the rationed foods we find two bananas, or even a bottle of Heinz 57 sauce."

They both chuckled over Lady Pratt's story of the little girl whose teacher asked her to draw a banana. The child drew a circle because she had never seen a banana.

In spite of the Pratt's privileges, however, Sir Frank had a problem. It irked him that the Labour government, which had replaced the Conservatives after the war, was trying to ease the plight of Britain's poorest. His income tax was nineteen shillings and sixpence in the pound (twenty shillings). And the "bloody government" was using his money to pay unemployed men on the dole two pounds ten shillings a week! Even worse, poor Orientals smuggled themselves into England, and went on the dole. They didn't try to get a job because the dole provided them with a life of luxury compared with their poverty-stricken lives at home.

The "bloody government" annoyed Sir Frank even more by using his tax money to provide free health services to anyone in Britain who wanted them. Pregnant women came over from the continent and had all their doctors' and hospital bills paid. Low-caste East Indians working on ships that docked in Britain got free spectacles and dentures. When they went home they sold them, and on subsequent trips they did the same thing.

Incidentally, Sir Frank scorned not only the lowly poor but also some of his cultural superiors. On one occasion, Bill and I mentioned that we had met a Mr. and Mrs. Macy. Mr. Macy was a high official in a firm of industrial consultants, and he and Mrs. Macy were returning to England after attending an international convention in the United States. We said that we found the Macys pleasant and cultured, but Sir Frank sniffed scornfully. From that point he kept referring to Mr. Macy as "a man who fixes roofs".

"Our company has no room for a man like that," he repeated emphatically.

Sir Frank didn't like Americans, either. He thought they were selfish.

"Their Marshall Plan helped Europe, yes. But it also helped the U.S. avoid a depression," he said.

Later he suggested that Canada should develop the St. Lawrence seaway project alone, then charge the U.S. "till it hurts".

Several other passengers agreed.

"We English are different from the Americans," a woman remarked later. "We don't have hardwood floors, but we don't try to keep up with the Joneses."

As we left the *Empress of France* about noon on Friday, June 29, and travelled by train from Liverpool to London, Bill and I were glad that the couple who shared our compartment were Mr. and Mrs. Macy. We chatted amiably as the small train sped past row after row after row of small houses in town after town. I felt the pressure of the crowded scene. Already I missed the openness of Canada.

In London we checked in at the Stafford Hotel, where accommodation had been arranged for us. The hotel, which was near St. James Palace in the heart of the city, exuded an air of unassuming luxury. Although it was near busy Piccadilly, it backed on Green Park, originally a royal preserve but now a beautiful public park. The staff welcomed us courteously and, best of all, the place was ideally quiet. Relieved and exhausted, we fell into the bed on which the covers had been turned down by one of the night maids.

At breakfast the next morning we were surprised to find that the austerity of rationing had not affected the Stafford's menu. It reminded me of the breakfasts I had read about in novels by P.G. Wodehouse and other English writers. There seemed to be unlimited juices, oranges, eggs boiled or scrambled, bacon, ham, kidneys, sausages, fried tomatoes and mushrooms, stewed fruit, marmalade, strawberry jam, hot rolls and toast, and an abundance of butter and cream.

When we had finished feasting, we sat in comfortable armchairs in the little waiting alcove off the dining room, letting our big meal digest before we went sightseeing. It was so early in the morning that the night porter was still on duty at the desk from which he directed guests to the dining room. As one approaching guest addressed him, my education was broadened.

The guest, I learned later, was Lady Millicent Somebody with a long hyphenated surname. She was wearing a bulky brown tweed suit and sturdy brown oxfords. She stood straight and tall, staring imperiously, not at the porter but at a place twelve inches above his head.

"My morning newspaper was not delivered," she proclaimed, frowning.

"I'm very sorry, my lady." The porter hurriedly checked something in his notebook. "I'm afraid your order was not recorded, my lady. I'm very sorry."

"Of course it was not recorded," Lady Millicent snapped. "I expect the hotel to do me the courtesy of delivering my newspaper without my having to order it!"

"Of course, my lady. We always try to please our guests." The porter looked penitent.

"Then attend to it immediately," Lady Millicent commanded the spot above the porter's head.

"Certainly, my lady," the porter murmured. "Immediately, my lady."

Lady Millicent marched past him toward the dining room. The head waiter bustled out to meet her. She nodded acknowledgement to this man who held a much higher position than the lowly night porter. Also, Bill and I noticed, she looked straight at him instead of at a spot above his head. But she didn't smile. The head waiter bowed low, then led her ladyship into the dining room.

"Oh, lord!" the porter groaned to the bellboy standing near the desk. "It's two years since she was last here. How do I know which paper she wants? And how can I find out without insulting her?"

"Blimey!" exclaimed the young bellboy who, we learned later, had been hired only a few days ago. "She's a real battle-axe, that one!"

"Don't you dare say such things!" The elderly porter frowned at the boy, who looked as if he had just left school at fourteen, and was working at his first job. "She's a real lady, that's what she is! A real lady!"

"I'm going to learn a lot while we're in England," I said to Bill.

We left the porter with his problem, and set out to see the sights of London.

TWENTY-NINE

We did our sightseeing on foot and while riding in the top sections of the double-decker buses, although I felt that Stafford guests rated a taxi. We saw such tourist attractions as The Mall, Buckingham Palace, Regent Street, Bond Street and its dozens of expensive shops, Threadneedle Street, and the Bank of England. We went as far as Shepherd's Bush, but our main point of interest was Canada House, in Trafalgar Square. There great flocks of pigeons fluttered about the statues of the lions, and some birds flew up to rest on top of Nelson's Column. Bill's office was in Canada House, but this was Saturday, and nobody was at work.

Our cultural treat came that evening, when we went to the small Arts Theatre for the third program of the Shaw Festival. I knew the play, but seeing it was infinitely more satisfying than reading it in my book of Shaw's plays.

Although the next day, Sunday, was July 1, the Canadian national holiday, any celebrations were scheduled for Monday. So we spent Sunday evening visiting the retired RCMP superintendent, who was so far removed from RCMP influence that he was known as Major Wright. He, his wife and their two friends seemed as anxious to warn us about the English situation as Sir Frank Pratt had been. They complained, as he had done, and added stories of women who queued up for an hour to get free aspirin for headaches, or cotton-wool for earaches rather than pay for those items.

On Monday afternoon we went to a reception at Canada House, by taxi this time as more suitable, to pay our respects to the Canadian High Commissioner, Dana Wilgress, and Mrs. Wilgress. Viscount and Lady Alexander and several other titled people were already there, but we didn't try to meet them.

Instead we toured Canada House, guided by RCMP Corporal Dalton, who was in charge of security there. Poor Dalton was thankful that Bill, an inspector, would have an office in Canada House. He hoped that Bill would have authority to improve the situation. Bill explained that his terms of reference didn't include the security of Canada House, and that Dalton should report his problems to the High Commissioner. If Dalton still had difficulties, however, Bill would discuss the matter with the High Commissioner.

Security, the corporal told us, was shockingly lax, but no one would pay any attention to his warnings. Diplomats' secretaries left secret files on their desks, and went out without locking their doors, while other employees were just as careless. The secretaries tore up classified documents and threw the pieces in their wastepaper baskets instead of in approved receptacles. Dalton had pieced some of the scraps together to make whole pages and so prove to the secretaries what could happen. But they still disposed of classified documents as before. And even if Canada House personnel did take the trouble to lock their doors, Dalton said, the fire escapes provided easy access to the offices.

Dalton's outburst eased his mind, and a more cheerful corporal came with us to an early dinner, another sumptuous feast at the Stafford.

During the meal my sympathy went out to Dalton and his wife, who had preferred to stay at home. She was his English war bride, and had found Mounted Police life in Canada extremely difficult. In the post-war shuffle of RCMP members, Dalton and his wife had endured eleven moves in four years. Mrs. Dalton, in poor health, longed to return to England, and when Dalton had a chance to take over security at Canada House, he did so. Now he longed to return to Canada, while his wife dreaded it. The situation seemed to have no happy resolution for a desperately unhappy couple.

After dinner Dalton took us sightseeing. This time we travelled in his little Morris Minor car, in which he had to shift gears manually and frequently. At each shift the little car gave a shudder and a forward jerk, which we found disconcerting. But we were grateful to Dalton.

Now we saw bombed sections of the city still in ruins, Lambeth, the Houses of Parliament, Downing Street and the Cenotaph. At the

Speakers' Corner in Hyde Park, three speakers standing on upturned barrels shouted their messages. One ranted against the Communists, a black man pleaded for better treatment of Negroes (only later called Blacks), while the third shouted about the need for religion in daily life. Three other religious speakers, one an ordained minister, stood on boxes nearby, all vying for the attention of the small crowd. Soon we pushed on again, with more shifting of shuddering gears, to Hampstead Heath, Dick Whittington's stone, St. Paul's Cathedral, and a dozen other places we'd only heard of or read about.

The next morning Bill went to his third-floor office in Canada House and worked there all day. I had no obligation to be useful, so I spent the morning walking about the London streets, where I found the shops full of unrationed luxury goods. Fortnum and Mason, which I as a Canadian thought of as a department store, seemed to have the widest variety and the most expensive of luxury goods. It was such a high-class emporium that clerks in the grocery department wore black formal suits, white shirts and high stiff white collars.

In the afternoon I went to a matinee of Chekov's *The Three Sisters*. I knew the play from reading it, but Celia Johnson, Diana Churchhill and Ralph Richardson gave it such full and vibrant life that I felt I was getting to know the real Chekov for the first time. At the intermission, anyone who ordered it was served tea, no matter where she sat. So I balanced a tray on my lap, thinking of Chekov's insight and the skill of the distinguished actors while I enjoyed a pot of tea, bread and butter, and a big slice of light fruitcake. Later I went home by way of Covent Garden, where I bought tickets for the current ballet. This was the kind of British culture I had anticipated!

Everything in London was fascinating, but we couldn't stay at the Stafford indefinitely, even though the RCMP was paying the bill. We must begin looking for more ordinary, less-expensive housing. First, though, I must find a chiropractor to ease my troublesome back. Bill chose one with a Welsh name and an office near Victoria Station. I made an evening appointment so that Bill could go with me.

As it turned out, Dr. Llewellyn was not Welsh, but Canadian. He had lived in Saskatchewan, homesteading, for twenty-five years. On the outbreak of war he had joined the army. After being shell-shocked early in the war, he stayed in England. Then he learned to be a chiropractor, and made a good living. But he was sick of England, its post-war scarcities, and especially its stifling class system. He longed to return to the freedom and the openness of Canada, but couldn't because he was not allowed to take any money out of the country. So, heartsick, he stayed.

He was overwhelmed with joy at meeting two Canadians who knew Saskatchewan intimately. He steadfastly refused to accept payment for my splendid first treatment, and was reluctant to let us leave. As we did so, his nurse, who looked undernourished and haggard, told us that she, too, longed to leave England. She hadn't enough money to buy nourishing food, she explained, and she was always tired.

For the rest of the week I visited (real) estate agents and looked at whatever living accommodation seemed promising, and Bill came with me in the evenings. All the available furnished flats were drab and dingy, with battered old furniture, and some flats were appallingly dirty. All were heated from fireplaces, most by gas, but some still used coal. Bill and I knew we must look for a flat or a house in an outlying district.

The next weekend we went by train to Wales to visit his parents, who of course welcomed us warmly. A steady stream of uncles, aunts, cousins and friends traipsed in and out of the house, all delighted to see us, and many of them asking when Bill was coming home to stay. They found it hard to believe that he had actually become a Canadian and enjoyed living in far-off Canada.

On Monday we began house hunting in earnest, in the evenings, on weekends, and on any afternoon when Bill felt he could spare the time. We travelled by underground, bus, train and taxi to the London suburbs and to towns near enough for Bill to commute to Canada House. Often Corporal Dalton, generous as earlier, drove us in his Morris Minor with the shuddering gear shift. As I had done in London, we visited estate agents and looked at dozens of "possibles".

For several weeks we had no luck, which upset Bill more than it upset me. After all, I spent my free time going to plays, visiting art galleries and museums, and visiting historic sites in London. By contrast, Bill had no free time. He was trying desperately to organize, from a distance, Mounted Police affairs on the continent. It worried him that he had to take time away from his work to look for housing. At the same time he was worried because he couldn't find a suitable home for me.

Several times we almost succeeded, but there was always some insurmountable drawback. We found a pleasant house at Wimbledon, but the owner wanted to use part of it as her own flat. Next we went by taxi to Windsor, where an estate agent directed us to The Friary. We had checked a map, and knew that the taxi driver was taking us a very long way off the direct route. We thought he was intent on charging a higher fare than he should have done.

"Here we are," he said at last. "This is The Priory." He quoted us an unusually high fare.

"I asked you to take us to The Friary," Bill said sharply.

"Oh, you Americans!" the taxi driver looked scornfully at Bill. "You Americans are always getting these two places mixed up."

So he drove us back to The Friary and charged another high fee. We didn't have any luck there, but we had a much shorter ride home with a different taxi driver.

Next we went to see Mrs. Clyne's house. It was big and beautiful, with a garden edged with lavender, and the prospect of a tame deer visiting it occasionally. But the only way of heating the house was by fireplaces, one in each of the eight rooms. So we moved on again.

Dalton drove us to Guildwood, Leatherhead and Dorking. We had no luck at any of those towns, although we saw a beautiful house to let. The owner was a man who had filled it with Oriental treasures amassed during his many travels. It was not too difficult to heat. We were ready to take it when the owner explained that he was going to live and work in Egypt, but for only nine months of each year.

Commander Thompson also had a lovely house, but wanted to rent it for one year only.

Mrs. Mills had a splendid house, not too difficult to heat, near London, and not far from Heathrow airport. Mrs. Mills led us out to look at her lovely garden, as splendid and well-tended as the house, and edged with graceful elms. As we stood admiring it, a small plane flew overhead. Mrs. Mills explained nonchalantly that she was not bothered by the aircraft. Only private planes used the airfield, she said, and even those flew infrequently. Then a huge passenger plane sped towards us with a thundering roar, drowning the rest of Mrs. Mill's soothing remarks. It flew dangerously low over Mrs. Mill's elms.

"Those damned planes!" she screamed, looking up at the sky and shaking her clenched fist. "One of these days they'll get caught in the trees and crash and serve them bloody well right!"

We moved on once more.

At last, after almost six weeks of house hunting in vain, we were lucky. The office of the Canadian High Commissioner had received word that a United Nations official had been transferred to Thailand (formerly Siam). He wanted to rent his house at Kingswood, Surrey, not far from London and with excellent train service. It was a modern house with central heating.

Mr. Cranzer, the United Nations official, took us to see it. To our amazement, it seemed as desirable as he had described it. Although the walls of the living room, dining room and kitchen were very dirty, he promised to have them repainted before we moved in. We agreed to rent White Oaks for two years, and learned that we could move in on September 19, the day the Cranzers would move out.

Only about a month to wait! Then we'd be comfortably settled! It was hard to believe!

THIRTY

Soon after we had arranged to rent White Oaks from Mr. Cranzer, Bill's health gave way. He saw a medical doctor, who diagnosed the trouble as stress, and recommended a Harley Street psychiatrist, Dr. Wiseman. On August 28, at that doctor's suggestion, Bill went for two weeks' rest at a convalescent home at Rustington, on the south coast. It was a quiet, secluded place where shell-shocked soldiers had recuperated during and after World War II.

I felt heartsick for Bill, who had always seemed to enjoy overworking and travelling incessantly as his various jobs demanded. On the other hand, I wasn't surprised that stress had at last overcome him. I believed that the past six weeks of nerve-racking inability to find suitable housing was the last straw, and that when we achieved it by chance, Bill's composure gave way.

Two days later, at Dr. Wiseman's request, I went to see him. I had allowed myself plenty of time to get from the Stafford to Harley Street, but somehow I got lost. I was so distressed that by the time I arrived, I had a severe headache.

My ringing of the outdoor bell was answered by a young woman in a white uniform. She ushered me into a big room with a deep-pile beige rug almost wall-to-wall. Somewhere near the door stood a three-foot model of a little black boy. It reminded me of the movie versions of black boys who held the horses' reins for old-time southern American gentleman at the front of Gone-with-the-Wind-type mansions. Dr. Wiseman's black boy held a tray level with his head, but I couldn't guess why. In any case the black boy looked grossly out of place. The big room had massive furnishings: settees, armchairs, a bookcase, a huge fireplace, and a big low table with bright picture books and *Punch* magazines.

The young woman led me to a small elevator, which ascended for one floor only. I walked up a steep flight of stairs to the third floor. It had probably been the sleeping area for many servants who had originally worked in that grand old house.

Dr. Wiseman met me at the open door. I entered a room with a powder-blue rug that had even deeper pile than the rug in the waiting room. Here the furnishings were also oversize, and here the grate of the massive marble fireplace held a glowing coal fire. I realized that now I was feeling the comforting warmth I had missed ever since leaving Canada.

The eminent psychiatrist sat behind his huge mahogany desk, and I sat opposite. He told me how dreadfully stressed Bill was from his demanding work over the years. Also, his travelling had been even more stressful because he had always felt he must hurry home to be with me and to please me. Dr. Wiseman made it sound as if Bill's breakdown was all my fault.

My headache was nagging me. Besides, I'd been so upset at getting lost and perhaps being late for my two o'clock appointment that I'd allowed myself only a chocolate bar for lunch. I had eaten it surreptitiously while hurrying along fashionable Regent Street. My headache prevailed over any possible intimidation. Rather sharply I enumerated some of my own problems over those same years. Then, regretting my impoliteness, I apologized.

"In spite of everything, I still love my husband," I said. "And I never would have complained, except that I have an overpowering headache."

"I believe it's a good thing you have a headache," a solicitous Dr. Wiseman assured me. "It made you talk frankly."

We parted amicably. I felt the warmth of his fire and his understanding, and went out into the early autumn chill of the sunless London streets.

A few days later, on September 2, I wrote in my journal: "No wonder Bill had to give in after twelve years of stress. Always work, work, work, travel, travel, travel. If he had cared for me less, it would have been better for him, but I appreciate that fact to the full, and I appreciate him the more for it. I hope he will lean on me now, as I have leaned on him."

In the middle of Bill's two weeks at Rustington I went there by train and stayed overnight. Bill greeted me warmly, but I could see he was shaky and uneasy. That night I lay beside him unable to settle down until his steady breathing indicated he was asleep. Whenever he turned over, I jerked out of my resting. When he wanted an aspirin, I was alert, ready to spring out of bed to get it for him. At last, after two o'clock, he seemed to sleep. But whenever I tried to sleep, I was disturbed by the thought that I was at least partly responsible for Bill's pitiable condition. Yet I couldn't bring him back to his normal bright, confident self. I could only wait for his natural recuperative powers to do that.

Back at the Stafford I wrote in my journal: "I would like to enfold him in my arms and shield him from disquiet as he has so long shielded me."

In an effort to keep from worrying, I filled my days with activity, but I worried even as I did so. I went several times to the British Museum and prowled about the Egyptian and Chinese rooms. I saw the Elgin Marbles, the Rosetta Stone and manuscripts by noted British writers. It encouraged me to see that a typescript by Freya Stark, the noted traveller, looked much like my own, with words and lines crossed out, and corrections made by hand. I went to Foyle's, the famous bookshop, and bought books by, and biographies of, such writers as Katherine Mansfield, Edith Wharton, Henry James, Tolstoy, H.G. Wells and Julian Huxley. I went to a matinee of Shaw's *Antony and Cleopatra*, starring Vivian Leigh and Lawrence Olivier. Miss Leigh was so devastatingly charming that I wrote in my journal, "Poor Antony".

In the evenings I read or listened to radio programs of the British Broadcasting Corporation. The Third Program, distinct from the Home and Light Services, was filled with talks and discussions about world affairs, the arts, famous plays, science, astronomy and so on.

At first I thought that the Third Program, which was broadcast from six o'clock every evening, indicated that the British were more cultured and intellectual than Canadians. We enjoyed such programs only once a week, on the Canadian Broadcasting Corporation's Wednesday Night programs. Later, however, the BBC's magazine, *The Listener*, carried a financial statement and a breakdown of listeners to its three separate services. It stated that of each twenty shillings (one pound) spent on the whole system, only one shilling and four pence was spent on the Third Program. Moreover, listeners to the Third Program were too few to be included in the statistics. Evidently Canadians were not too far behind, if at all.

At the end of Bill's two weeks at Rustington, I went there again, this time to accompany him back to London. On arriving at the

Stafford, we learned that we must move to a smaller room, as ours had been reserved for another guest earlier in the year.

At first the maid complained about having to help me move to the smaller room. Then she complained about the difficulty of cleaning it because our two big wardrobe trunks took up so much space. Finally she protested vigorously at having to dust Bill's numerous medicine and pill bottles. I had always been friendly, as I was with everyone. But now I lost my temper.

"It's not my fault we had to change rooms," I snapped. "And it's not my fault we have to live in a hotel for three months. As for my husband's medicines, he's sick and he needs them all. Now do the cleaning! And don't you dare complain about my husband's medicines or anything else!"

The maid must have thought I'd turned into a Lady Millicent type, used to having subservient service. In any case, I certainly went up in her estimation. From that moment she not only stopped complaining, but she also cleaned thoroughly, and thanked me each time for allowing her to do so.

At last, on the afternoon of Wednesday, September 19, we went by train and taxi to White Oaks, Sandy Lane, Kingswood, near Tadworth, Surrey, about seventeen miles south of London.

Bill paid our taxi driver, and we went indoors. The Cranzers were still there, with only one hour left to catch their plane to Bangkok. The scene was utter confusion. The Cranzers were paying the telephone bill, the laundry bill and the gas bill. They were also telephoning friends to say goodbye, and at the same time stuffing things into brown paper bags. Mr. Cranzer, a short, stocky Czechoslovakian, was also supervising his waiting taxi driver's loading of suitcases, brown paper bags, and assorted packages tied with string. Meanwhile, two-year-old Johnny ran out and in, shrieking with excitement, and kicking everything he ran past, but completely ignored by his parents.

At one point Mrs. Cranzer, short like her husband and rather plump, paused in her frenetic activity in the living room and turned her attention to me.

"Life with a child is not easy," she declared. "Hilda, my live-in maid, had no time to do anything but look after the child and do the cooking. It was very difficult for me."

I thought it would have been better if Hilda had stayed to supervise the child until the Cranzers left White Oaks.

Then Mrs. Cranzer confided that she knew that Bill and I, with no children, would take good care of the place.

Later we learned that Mr. Cranzer had agreed to rent the house to an American diplomat with four children. But when we, a childless couple, wanted it, he reneged on his agreement with the four-child American and rented White Oaks to us. When we heard that interesting news from the real estate agent in charge of the rental, I thought of the Cranzer child. Probably it was Johnny's behaviour that had led his father to rent White Oaks to us. We owed a lot to Johnny.

Soon we stood outside, watching the Cranzers drive away in their taxi. As they turned from our driveway into Sandy Lane, the child leaned far out of the open window, still shrieking incessantly, still ignored by his parents.

We hadn't yet gone back into the house when a postman rode up on his bicycle.

"These are for Mr. Cranzer," he said, dismounting and taking two big parcels from his carrier basket. Immediately we noticed an unpleasant odour, as if something had decayed.

"Mr. Cranzer and his family have moved," Bill explained. "Our name is Kelly, and we are his tenants. You'll have to send his mail on to his forwarding address."

The postman looked worried. "Mr. Cranzer didn't leave a forwarding address," he said, " and he gets these parcels all the time. Shall I leave them with you, sir?"

I had backed away from the postman and his smelly delivery, but Bill moved close enough to examine the labels. Apparently Mr. Cranzer had not only neglected to leave a forwarding address. He had neglected to cancel the food deliveries that eked out his ration allowances. Bill saw that the parcel with the overwhelming bad smell contained a ham from Holland. The other held rye bread from Glasgow, Scotland.

"You'll have to take the parcels back to the post office," Bill said firmly.

Reluctantly the postman put the parcels back in his basket, then mounted his bicycle and rode away.

Before we went indoors, Bill and I inspected our "estate", admiring everything. The house, ultra-modern in England in the early 1950s, had a flat roof that added to the impression of a big cube covered with gleaming white stucco. Its many large windows, some ordinary, some walk-through French windows, seemed perfectly suitable for the stark white structure that stood on three-quarters of an acre of well-tended grounds.

Spiky red flowers with abundant dark green leaves had been planted all around the house, close to the white walls. And the charming dwelling was surrounded by velvety green lawns and multicoloured flower beds. At the back of the house there was even a graceful latticework archway covered with climbing roses. Rows of cedars sheltered a vegetable garden where stalks of Brussels sprouts stood waiting to be stripped. Scattered about the lawns and edging the driveway, sturdy oaks towered skyward.

"It's a wonderful place," I said to Bill. "We never could have afforded to pay the whole rent ourselves."

"Never," Bill agreed. And I knew that both of us were thinking of the "perks" that came with his new job. A generous overseas allowance had been added to Bill's annual RCMP salary of $3,000, and the Force was paying half our rent.

Later we heard the unhappy story of our unusual house and its attractive surroundings. A young English architect, we learned, had lived and worked in India for several years. Before returning to England he had married a beautiful Indian girl, and had designed White Oaks as a perfect setting for his lovely young wife. After living there for a short time, the ideally happy couple learned that the young woman was pregnant with the child they eagerly desired. However, both mother and child died in childbirth. The husband, in the anguish of his bereavement, immediately sold the house. He was never again seen in Kingswood, and rumour had it that he had perhaps returned to India.

As we continued to explore outdoors, we saw, between the house and the garage, a small room below ground level. It housed a furnace and a coal bin. The furnance would provide us with central heating by way of hot water in oversize radiators, about three feet high and four feet long.

A service manual hanging near the coal-burning furnace explained the operation of the only such furnace we heard of while we lived in England. It was lit with a gas poker. The coal, bean-size, went into a hopper on top of the firebox only once a day and dropped in automatically. The burning produced no ashes, only one big klinker to be taken out each morning with a pair of tongs.

"What a treasure," I said, thinking of all the fireplace-heated places we'd seen.

"And you won't even have to tend it," Bill smiled. "I'm sure I can get someone to look after it when I'm away."

I felt sure he was right. We already had a part-time gardener, and the prospect of a cleaning woman. Mr. Cranzer had arranged for Mr. Killick, his twice-a-week gardener, to carry on as before. And Mr. Killick in turn had said that his sister-in-law, Mrs. Marie (pronounced Marry) Harding, would agree to be our cleaning woman. Everything was working out splendidly!

We went indoors, and I persuaded Bill to rest while I made a pot of tea. He had still not completely recovered from his illness, but he had been granted three weeks holiday to help him get back to normal. It was his first three weeks off duty since July 1939, when we had gone from Saskatchewan to Toronto to get advice about Bill's chance of a singing career, and to find help for my troublesome back.

Of course we had seen most of the house with Mr. Cranzer before we rented it. But we had been so eager to lease what seemed like an ideal place for us that we hadn't paid much attention to the details. Now, as I went into the kitchen, I noticed that it was very small and inconvenient, much more suitable for an English maid than her mistress. Also, it had a gas stove without a pilot light. But I didn't care. I lit the stove with a match and ignored the great flame that swooshed out at me, and the lingering faint smell of gas. Soon I had a tray of tea and biscuits to take to Bill in the living room.

The big living and dining rooms were also disappointing. Mr. Cranzer hadn't kept his promise to have the dirty walls repainted. The burlap-like floor covering, like all the upholstered and wooden furniture, was dark and brown. Moreover, the foliage of the mature oak trees kept the minimal English light from brightening the rooms. But I still didn't care! I was thankful to be at White Oaks!

After tea Bill came to look at the kitchen, and there I had some pleasant surprises. A narrow inner door opened onto a big pantry with plenty of shelves. Another door led to a small room. It had probably been a maid's room, but now it housed a huge American refrigerator and an old-fashioned treadle sewing machine. The refrigerator meant that I wouldn't have to go shopping as often as I'd feared. The sewing machine would let me do what I enjoyed. The first thing I'd do with it would be to finish my pretty pink dress. Of course I couldn't know it at the time, but that was the dress I would wear at our first garden party at Buckingham Palace.

A few moments later we went upstairs, and again I was pleasantly surprised. All the rooms were big and bright, and the bedrooms had deep-piled, wall-to-wall carpeting in light green. As a plus, the master bedroom had a huge bay window with French doors leading to a big balcony built over the garage. The bay window was completely lined with the same oversize radiators as those in all the rooms except the kitchen. Through its windows I could look up between the tree tops and see the sky! I knew where I would spend much of my time when Bill was away!

One big bright room, Mr. Cranzer had told us, was the original nursery. Its floor was bare, probably in the cause of less dust and fewer germs. I decided at once to use it as my writing room. As soon as my IBM electric typewriter and my big folding table were delivered from storage, I would buy the necessary transformer and begin writing.

"I'm going to like living here," I said to Bill as we went back to the master bedroom and both of us stretched out on the big comfortable bed for a much-needed rest.

We spoke of pleasures to come, one of them the car Bill had ordered, a Ford Consul, which was in London ready for us to pick up. New cars were still hard to get in that post-war period. We probably received preferred treatment because payment for the car originated in very welcome Canadian dollars.

Bill had learned that he would be expected to attend the next Interpol convention, to be held in Stockholm, Sweden, the following spring. "And of course you'll come with me," he smiled.

Corporal Dalton had told us that Bill's position would entitle us to an invitation to the Royal garden party at Buckingham Palace each year Bill was at Canada House.

"And I want you to fly with me to as many places as you like," Bill said. "How would you like to come to Paris, and Rome, and Athens, and a dozen other main cities in Europe?"

"I'd love to," I responded warmly. And I thought to myself that my two years in England, plus visits to all those other fascinating places, would no doubt give me enough material for my next book.

Then I thought of the earlier difficulties I'd endured because I loved my mountie. Some memories were still painful; the ache of waiting for the RCMP to allow us to marry; the unfulfilled longing to enjoy more time with Bill during the first years of our married life; the torment of being bombarded with noise as I struggled to write my first Mounted Police history while living in Ottawa. Most painful of all was the remembered hell of Fredericton, where my expectation of a companionable life with Bill had been shattered.

How different things would be now! Of course Bill would be away a lot, but I could go with him whenever I wished. And when I chose to stay at home I'd be comfortable, in a lovely, quiet house in a beautiful, quiet setting, with home help indoors and out. Best of all, Bill was well on the way to complete recovery from his illness.

I snuggled up to him. "I'm tired but very happy," I said.

"I'm tired and very happy, too," Bill murmured, and held me close.

I smiled as I thought of pleasures the future held for my mountie and me. Then, although it was still afternoon, I drifted from happy anticipation into the deep sleep of contentment.